Arguments fo...

D1335015

80p

Series editor: John Harrison

Arguments for Socialism is a new series of popular and provocative books which deal with the economic and political crisis in Britain today. The series argues the need for a radical rethinking of major political questions and contributes to the debates on strategy for the left.

'One of the main reasons why the Tories swept to power in 1979 was that the Labour movement had over the years almost ceased to argue for socialism. This new series, *Arguments for Socialism*, can play a significant part in re-establishing the necessity for a socialism that is democratic, libertarian and humane.' *Tony Benn*

Getting It Together

Women as Trade Unionists

Jenny Beale

Pluto  Press

First published 1982 by Pluto Press Limited,
Unit 10 Spencer Court,
7 Chalcot Road,
London NW1 8LH

British Library Cataloguing in Publication Data
Beale, J.
Getting it together: women as trade unionists.—(Arguments for socialism)
1. Women in trade unions—Great Britain
I. Title   II. Series
331.4'0941   HD6079.2G7
ISBN 0 86104 500 9

Designed by Clive Challis A Gr R
Typeset by Promenade Graphics Limited,
Block 23a Lansdown Industrial Estate, Cheltenham GL51 8PL
Printed and bound in Great Britain
by Richard Clay (The Chaucer Press) Ltd, Bungay, Suffolk

Contents

Abbreviations

ACTT	Association of Cinematograph, Television and Allied Technicians
APEX	Association of Professional, Clerical and Computer Staffs
ASTMS	Association of Scientific, Technical and Managerial Staffs
AUEW	Amalgamated Union of Engineering Workers
CIS	Counter Information Services
COHSE	Confederation of Health Service Employees
CPSA	Civil and Public Services Association
GMWU	General and Municipal Workers Union
NALGO	National and Local Government Officers Association
NATFHE	National Association of Teachers in Further and Higher Education
NUJ	National Union of Journalists
NUPE	National Union of Public Employees
NUT	National Union of Teachers
SOGAT	Society of Graphical and Allied Trades
SR	*Spare Rib*
TGWU	Transport & General Workers Union
USDAW	Union of Shop, Distributive and Allied Workers
WV	*Women's Voice*

For Janet Miller with love and thanks

Acknowledgements

I owe a great deal to the many women who as friends, students and members of women's groups, have taught me about women's lives. My special thanks to the women shop stewards whose thoughts have helped this book to come alive and to other women tutors for our work together. A very warm thank you to Eva Kaluzynska for encouraging me to write and for her help, to Jane Wheelock and Simon Henderson for their comments on the draft, to John Harrison for helpful editing, to Johanna Fawkes for detailed work on the final manuscript, to the women who so generously agreed to be interviewed: Lillian Dunwoodie, Barbara Gunnell, Ellen Parker and Harriet Vyse, and, once again, to Eva Kaluzynska who conducted and wrote up the interview with Barbara Gunnell. Many others have given me support and encouragement: Doug Miller and my colleagues at Newcastle Poly; everyone at Brookside; Ann, Martin and Dee Beale and Colin Brown.

Preface

What is it like to be a woman trade unionist? How has the women's movement influenced the unions? What *is* women's work? And have we learned anything from the long struggle for equality? I set out to answer these questions in a tone of celebration rather than a moan. It is, of course, true that women still lack power in unions. Many things hold us back, from sexism and domestic ties to the restrictions of part-time work. But women also enrich trade unionism. We bring into unions our own strong traditions of action and a challenge to present-day priorities. We made an important contribution in the past, and we may be a crucial force in the near future by helping to re-shape trade unions into a form appropriate to the late twentieth century. I hope this book will encourage both women and men to take more pride in our achievements as women and trade unionists.

Recently, many people on the left have been trying to forge a more popular, accessible socialism out of the aims and aspirations of apparently disparate political groupings. I hope this book will play its own small part in this development in two ways—by exploring the overlap between women's politics and trade unionism and by showing how supposedly 'female' areas of life, such as health, housework and childcare, are important concerns for all trade unionists.

Much of this book has grown out of my work as a trade union tutor in the West of Scotland and Newcastle upon Tyne. I have relied on quotes from many fantastic women I have had the pleasure of teaching on shop stewards' course to illustrate the experiences of working women in their unions. The four portraits are also an important part of the book. The women involved work in widely different jobs: Ellen is a clerk, Lillian is a hospital cleaner, Barbara works in journalism and Harriet was an engineering worker. Their personal experiences—so different, yet with so many themes in common—

speak volumes about the issues many of us face as women, as trade unionists, or as both.

Jenny Beale
April 1982

1.

'Are We Downhearted? No!'

In the summer of 1911, conditions in the jam and pickle-making factories in Bermondsey became almost unbearable. The weather was unusually hot, and boiling vats of liquid caused temperatures inside the factories to soar even higher. Weekly wages were as low as seven shillings, and very few of the women workers belonged to a union.

One morning in August, the women in a big confectionary factory suddenly left work and started to march down the street. As they passed by, other workers came out to see what was happening and joined in. Women from jam and biscuit factories, tea packing houses and glue works marched together in a singing, laughing procession.

No-one knew exactly how the protest had started, but soon there were over a thousand women out on strike in 20 separate disputes—all demanding more money. Mary Macarthur, the organiser of the Women's Trade Union League, realised the urgent need to support the strikers. She quickly set up a headquarters in Bermondsey and appealed to the public for help. £500 was donated within the week, and bread and milk were distributed. Processions marched daily through the City of London with collecting boxes. The *Daily Chronicle* reported that a mass meeting in Southwark Park was attended by 15,000 men and women:

> The women seemed to be in the highest spirits. They went laughing and singing through Bermondsey shouting 'Are we downhearted?' and answering the question by a shrill chorus of 'No!' It was noticeable that many of them had put on their 'Sunday best'. In spite of the great heat, hundreds of them wore fur boas and tippets—the sign of self-respect.

Within three weeks, 18 of the 20 strikes ended in victory, and 4,000 women had joined a union for the first time. The *Women's Trade*

Union Review recorded in October 1911 that the greatest gain had been 'the new sense of self-reliance, solidarity and comradeship . . . making it certain that, whatever the difficulties and dangers of the future, they will never again be, like those of the past, without hope'.

The history of women in trade unions is rich with events such as the Bermondsey strike. They underline the fact that women need unions for the same reasons as men do—to protect and improve conditions at work and as a force for social and political change. Individual workers have always been weak against the power of employers and the state. The rallying cry of 'Unity is Strength' is as relevent today as it was in 1911. The need for trade unions has not diminished over the years. Today, living standards are threatened once again by industrial decline and unemployment. Working conditions for many are still a problem. In 1979, a woman called Sharojben Patel told *Spare Rib* about the factory where she worked:

> Conditions at Futters are degrading. Racial abuse is very common. There is only one toilet upstairs for 40 workers and it is rarely cleaned. There is no drinking water, just a dirty old sink. There is no sick pay . . . and no protective clothing, not even gloves when you have to work with your hands in oil. (*SR* 81)

Other workers at the plant, a light engineering factory, said that pregnant women had been forced to do heavy manual work, and that women who 'answered back' had to work on dangerous machines.

Many women still do hard, dangerous, exhausting work. New industries create new problems too. Keyboard operators suffer headaches and eye-strain; radiation can be a hazard in hospitals and laboratories; and fast, mindless assembly jobs produce stress. Joining a union and using the strength of collective action is still the only effective way of fighting for a change at work. For women in large factories or local authorities the union plays a vital role in negotiating wages and conditions, and representing individuals. In small, scattered workplaces such as shops, hairdressers and clothing factories, the need for protection is often greater, though union organisation is more difficult.

Recently, women have fought a number of bitter disputes over the right to join a union in small factories with appalling conditions and anti-union employers. Futters was one example. Over half the women joined the engineering union, the AUEW, and went on strike when the manager refused to recognise the union. The Grunwick dispute in 1977 was another. The workers, mostly Asian women, struck for union recognition. They had joined the clerical union APEX in a desperate attempt to improve their pay of £28 for a 40-hour week. They were also determined to stop the arbitrary imposition of overtime—a nightmare to mothers with children in school or nursery.

Unionisation was a courageous move. As one worker said, 'They harass you so much in there that you couldn't think of joining a trade union'. Jayaben Desai, who emerged as a leader of the strike, interviewed by *Spare Rib*, described how she began to realise how important trade unions were:

> I realised that the workers are the people who give their blood for the management and that they should have good conditions, good pay and should be well-fed. The trade unions are the best thing here—they are not so powerful in other countries. They are a nice power, and we should keep it on.

The Grunwick strike became a symbolic struggle for the whole labour movement as workers from all over the country flocked to the picket lines. It was also a women's struggle. The mass pickets were unusual not only for their size but also for the sight of miners and steel workers linking arms with feminists, many of whom had never before been involved in industrial action.

At the moment, trade unions are relatively weak as the recession continues and unemployment soars. Women are an easy scape-goat at such times. Some people question women's right to work. Others mutter that married women should be the first to go when redundancies are declared. It is necessary to contradict this by stressing the enormous contribution women make to trade unionism.

Women do not only contribute in terms of numbers. They also widen the scope of trade union activity by introducing a number of important issues. And many women are challenging the way trade unions are organised. They are raising questions about union democracy which have an important bearing on the future of the trade union movement.

Strength in numbers

First of all, unions *are* the men and women in membership. One in three trade unionists is female. Without women the trade union movement would be smaller and weaker. Two-thirds of new recruits in the last twenty years have been female, as women's employment has increased and many traditional areas of men's work have declined.

But unions need more than passive members. They need active commitment. Women, like men, contribute vast amounts of energy, time and dedication to the cause. Women like Joyce Golding, striking for equal pay at Bronx Engineering in 1976:

> We have got to fight. It's not only for ourselves we have got to make this effort, but for future generations of women in this factory. Otherwise women will always stay in the position they are. (*SR* 44)

Women do not always fight just for themselves. They are conscious of their role within the wider movement. At the Lee Jeans factory in Greenock, for example, the workers mounted an occupation in February 1981 to stop the company closing it down. One woman explained: 'We are making a stand against companies like this, companies who make obscene profits and to hell with those they throw on the scrap heap' (CIS). Their initiative was applauded by a shop steward from the nearby Linwood plant of Talbot cars, itself under threat of closure, who said, 'These women are fighting for all of us'.

So unions and women need each other. Women are workers and a workforce that is divided is weaker than one that is united. Mary Carlin's words, written in the Transport and General Workers Union's *Record* in 1925, still hold true: 'Let us again remind our fathers and brothers in the union that the unorganised and low-paid woman worker is the greatest impediment to their advance.' In other words, *all* workers stand to gain from women being well-organised, active trade unionists. In practice, sexual divisions often weaken unions. Women and men tend to do different jobs, and compete with each other in the pursuit of sectional interests. Sexist attitudes within trade unions can make this worse. Some men still think women workers are less important than themselves. They under-rate women's potential power, and they are unwilling to give up their own privileged position. The result is that employers can exploit this lack of solidarity to their own advantage.

In spite of job losses, women are likely to continue to be the main source of new members for the trade unions. It has never been more important to recognise women's contribution, and for both women and men to encourage women's activity in trade unions, for the sake of the whole movement.

Women — a force for democracy?

Women hold the possibility of being a great force for democracy in the trade unions; a force which could make unions more responsive to the membership, more caring and more co-operative. A far-fetched claim? Well, let's look at the evidence.

It is almost a commonplace to say that unions today are dominated by bureaucracies. The larger unions in particular have developed complex hierarchies. Branches send delegates to trade groups and divisional councils, which in turn feed into regional councils and national committees. How many union members know what all these bodies do, or who sits on them? How many attend their branch meetings—the foundation stones of the whole structure? Debates about democracy rage in most unions. Members question the tenure of general secretaries and the power of executives, and complain about the lack of attention given to the grass roots.

Women are important in this debate in specific ways. The scarcity of women in the upper echelons of most unions is in itself a challenge to the existing structures. Are women at fault, or do the unions themselves present barriers to women's participation? If so, are there any alternatives? British trade unionism is dominated by traditions hammered out by skilled craftworkers in the shipyards and engineering shops of the nineteenth century. Women—along with black workers, young workers and unemployed sisters and brothers—are beginning to question these traditions. Are they appropriate to the service industries and offices of the late twentieth century? Do they cater for the interests of women workers?

If we look at who takes decisions in unions, we find that most important positions are held by men. Women are under-represented in a number of ways:

Women are almost entirely absent from national negotiations Something is surely wrong with democratic representation when the basic working conditions of thousands of women workers are negotiated by men. The wages of one in three manual workers and nearly half of all non-manual workers are negotiated at a national level. This includes most women working in the public sector, from school cleaners to social workers. Another third of manual workers, including most employees in engineering, have their basic hours and wages determined nationally through negotiations between the unions and employers' federations. These are then topped up by locally agreed payments and bonuses.

Yet there are virtually no women on any of the major negotiating committees—the bodies such as the Whitley Councils, the Burnham Committee and the Confederation of Shipbuilding and Engineering

Unions. The question is simply this: can male-dominated negotiating teams properly represent the needs and aspirations of women workers? Or do they tend to give priority to the things men think are important?

Few women hold high office in unions   There is a general rule that applies to all the main unions: the higher you go, the fewer women you find. Even the unions with substantial female memberships have a low proportion of women at every level above shop stewards. (See Chapter 2) Is there not something undemocratic about unions in which women are severely under-represented on decision-making bodies, and therefore in policy formation?

Women lose out over sectional interests   Every union aims to look after the interests of its own members. As a result, groups of workers are frequently thrown into competition with each other. This pursuit of sectional interests has always contradicted the ideal of unity among working people. It may divide union from union, as when a skilled union tries to increase its differential over the semi-skilled. Or the division may be between workers in the same union. Head teachers, for example, are paid out of the same purse as primary school teachers, but are on a different pay scale and earn much higher salaries. Nursing administrators get a larger slice of the cake than nurses. In both cases women lose out. Differences in status and skill usually follow sex lines, with women concentrated in the lower status, low-paid jobs. Differentials are often, therefore, maintained by men at women's expense.

Women's interests are not given priority   Questioning the need for differentials is an example of women challenging traditional negotiating priorities. This can be difficult, especially when the higher-paid workers are in the same union. One college lecturer expressed her frustration like this:

> I think it is terrible that heads of department are earning about £15,000, and are then claiming large sums in travelling expenses while women part-time lecturers are told there is no work for them because of the cuts. To me it is immoral, but I can't say anything or my branch officials tell me I am not being a 'good trade unionist' as I am attacking the wages and conditions of our members. I think it is time we re-thought our priorities.

Another traditional practice challenged by low-paid women is that of claiming percentage increases. Flat-rate increases are preferred by the low paid as they could help to reduce differentials. After all, 10 per cent of £15,000 is a much larger sum than 10 per cent of £5,000—

it works out at about £20 a week more. The National Union of Public Employees (NUPE) made much of this in a campaign against low pay. It is now NUPE policy to negotiate across-the-board pay increases, and to prevent women being isolated on the lower grades by lessening or removing differentials.

Women are also questioning the priority given to the 'family wage'. This is the assumption that men need a wage large enough to support a family whereas women do not. Women's wages are regarded as secondary, as a supplement to the family income. This idea has dominated bargaining since the early days of trade unions and is still dominant today. This is despite the enormous increase in women in the workforce and the fact that most women's wages are not 'extras' but essential to their families. Ask women whether they work for pin-money and you will get some fairly angry replies:

That's rubbish. My family couldn't live without my wages.

My husband is unemployed, so how else would we live?

I used to work for pin-money, but not now. The cost of living is far too high.

If you call electricity, food and clothes 'extras', then I work for extras.

According to one estimate, the loss of women's wages would force another million families below the poverty line. Fewer than one working man in five is now the sole supporter of a wife and children, so the idea that men are the true breadwinners is hopelessly out of date.

How could all this help to democratise the unions? The possibility lies in women's approach to these problems. By challenging differentials and sectional interests, women could help to overcome these entrenched divisions between workers. There has been a recent burst of interest in positive action to boost women's participation in unions which is helping to redress the imbalance in representation. (See Chapter 7) The measures range from special women's seats on union executives to women's advisory committees and women-only training courses. All these give women a chance to discuss *their* priorities and *their* interests. The old controversy about whether women's conferences and committees are useful or divisive seems to be settling down a little as it is more widely accepted that they play a vital role in getting more women into union structures.

These are important steps towards more democratic representation, but they are not the whole story. Women are also raising the question of *how* things are done. A woman in the National Union of Teachers (NUT) expressed her concern like this:

> When I go to union meetings they are always in a big hall, and all the business is done by just a few people. I think it would be much better if we could run them differently. I'd like to talk to people about the work we do and about what's really going on in the classroom, rather than just hear about wage claims. It depends what you think unions are for, I suppose.

A similar feeling was expressed by women from NUPE on a shop stewards' course in Newcastle. To them, the formal structure of meetings was confusing and unnecessary (at least at branch level), and union jargon was often unintelligible. Two home helps described how they had changed their own branch. They had open, informal agendas and no standing orders or formal procedures. They always took time to introduce new members and called each other by their ordinary names. They held social events, and met in each other's houses or places within easy reach, rather than in pubs or clubs. If women had children, the branch would pay baby-sitting expenses.

These sound like simple measures. But if they were widely adopted they could dramatically change the traditional way of organising in a movement based largely on formality, procedure and committee rules. These have their place, but are they really necessary at all levels? Couldn't a more open organisation make union activity more accessible to *all* its members?

Ideas from the women's liberation movement have also made a considerable impact. Feminist trade unionists experience a sharp contrast between formal union business and the more flexible style of women's meetings. The women's movement has evolved in a way many trade unionists find quite baffling. A powerful social movement without leaders, without expensive London offices, without committees, without delegate meetings . . . impossible! At its best, the women's movement offers a real alternative. It has demonstrated the value of consciousness-raising, of giving each woman the space for her politics to grow out of her own, and other women's, experience. Ideas shape and develop as discussion flows between analysis and experience, emotion and intellect. Women learn to listen to each other, sharing feelings and ideas and understanding the need for mutual support.

> When I first became part of a consciousness-raising group, I didn't know that it would change my life. We were able to talk

about the conflicts in our lives and start really thinking about how we lived. I was no longer an individual with a few odd ideas, but a woman who became strong from being with other women. (*SR* 92)

Saturday was the most fantastic day of my life. I've never been to a women's conference before. It was amazing to be in a building surrounded by strong, open, loving women. (*SR* 58)

There *is* organisation in the women's movement. There are local networks of groups, women's centres, conferences, writing and publishing groups, and larger ventures like Women's Aid and Rape Crisis Centres. All very different to trade unionism, and the women involved in both movements have to live daily with the contradictions between them. Part of the value of women's committees and courses in unions is that they provide an area of overlap. In them, women can sometimes shed the formality of union procedures and TUC-speak and create a more supportive atmosphere in which to discuss their business.

Taking some of the experience of the women's movement into trade unions in this way could make an enormous difference. It could open up union structures and start to replace hierarchies with co-operation, remoteness with understanding. Making unions, in fact, more democratic. But this is very threatening to established interests in the movement. Will women's ways be allowed to grow, or will they be crushed and squeezed out?

The women's movement has had a profound influence on another sphere of union activity. Many issues first debated within women's groups have expanded the agenda of union thought and action. Let's turn now to how this has come about.

Women enrich trade unionism

Women bring into trade unions a rich political history of their own—the history of the struggles to live their lives in the way they want. Women have always taken issues from their own organisations into unions and political parties to give them as wide a base as possible. The suffragettes, for instance, reached out to women wherever they could. They held 'Votes for Women' meetings in factories and mills, in church halls and at streetcorners. Women raised the debate in every kind of political organisation.

A more up-to-date example is the campaign against cuts in the welfare state. This is a powerful cause for women. Every nursery closure means more work for mothers at home, and every shut-down of a geriatric ward forces individuals, usually women, to take over the caring. Local attempts to prevent closures have often turned into community issues where the workers have been joined by tenants' groups and women's groups to form action committees and organise protests.

In this way the line between women's action and trade-union action is often blurred. The one informs and enriches the other. Trade-union leaders, however, have sometimes been slow to acknowledge this. In his address to the TUC women's conference in 1972, Vic Feather tried to draw a distinction between trade-union women and the activists of the women's liberation movement:

> You cannot pick up a newspaper nowadays, even the most staid, without finding comments on women and the problems of women. I am not at all sure that some of the antics are helping women towards equality . . . What is needed is the sort of work you are doing. It is the sustained, persistent determination of trade-union women that will bring about a greater measure of equality.

He undoubtedly underestimated the degree of overlap between the two movements, and the value of some of the 'antics'. Although by no means all women in trade unions would define themselves as feminists, few activists would deny the influence of ideas from the women's movement or the inspiration they derive from women's struggles in the past.

Without active women to take up the issues in trade unions, would we have seen a campaign for equal pay? Or maternity leave? These are sometimes dismissed as 'women's issues'. But if we look a little more closely at what this means, we find that the issues are far from narrow. Take maternity rights, for example. This does not only refer to the rights of mothers to some time off work when their babies are born. It also raises questions about how our society values the care of babies and children, and the need for mothers and fathers to make real choices as to how they organise their time between their work and their families.

It is time to challenge the view that 'women's issues' are fringe matters because they do not concern men. Caring about traditionally 'female' areas of life should be an important part of trade unionism. This is not, of course, a new idea. Dora Russell is an example of a life-long feminist who believed that women should not play down their role as defenders of life, or deny their concern for personal relations, but should take credit for them. She agreed with the view held by some suffragettes that 'the entry of women into political life would bring a fresh and important contribution', and went on to say that she 'couldn't see any point in fighting to get women into politics if they were just the same as men'.

The women's movement has built on this view. The press has often suggested that women's liberation means women wanting to be like men. This is a mis-interpretation. It misses the point that women strive to free themselves from the things that oppress them so that they can live fuller lives *as women*. An important step in this process, and one that affects trade unionism, is the understanding that many aspects of people's personal lives are, in fact, political. The way we bring up our children, our relationships with other people and our health are all shaped by political forces and may need political action to change them.

Feminists have taken this understanding into trade unions by arguing that issues like abortion are legitimate subjects for trade-union action. Although they have met both incredulity and resistance at times, real advances have been made in some areas.

Abortion

Since the 1967 Abortion Act, there have been a number of attempts in parliament to restrict abortion rights. The most recent was a private members bill introduced by John Corrie in 1979. The feminist National Abortion Campaign led a strong opposition to the bill. In October 1979, a massive demonstration against the bill took place in London. It was organised by the TUC—the first time the trade union movement had called out its members on a social issue of this kind. This achievement was the result of years of vigorous campaigning by women in unions. They took the issue to the TUC women's conference, and later to full congress, where the TUC adopted a pro-abortion policy.

Women argued that abortion, like maternity rights, is not a narrow 'women's issue'. It is a trade-union matter because it affects the right of every working woman to exert control over her own life. Also, the demand for National Health Service abortion facilities to meet women's needs is closely linked to trade-union support for the welfare state. The issue affects men too, as fathers, husbands and lovers.

So it was no accident that the TUC organised the demonstration against the Corrie bill. As a member of the National Abortion Campagn explained:

We positively fought for a TUC demonstration because we

believed that it was the best way of bringing together the widest number of people to oppose the Corrie bill . . . The TUC is the most efficient, far reaching and adequately funded organisation for this and we are proud to be the first abortion movement in the world to get such trade union backing. (*SR* 89)

The march had its problems on the day, when a row broke out over who was to lead the sixty thousand or so demonstrators. But overall it was a remarkable coming together of two powerful social forces—the women's movement and the trade-union movement.

Images of women

Naked women draped across sports car ads, page three pin-ups, descriptions of women as 'blonde corkers' and 'sexy super-girls': there are endless examples of the way women's bodies and women's lives are distorted and misused in the media. A trade union issue? Yes, especially in the unions whose members write and publish such sexist material. The issue exploded in the National Union of Journalists (NUJ) in 1976, when the union's Equality Working Party published a pamphlet called *Images of Women in the Media*, which contained many examples of sexism and offered suggestions for good practice. Although a review in the union's own newspaper recommended the publication as 'sound reading for every journalist', three letters and a back-page columnist disagreed. 'At first I laughed', wrote one. 'Then I wondered how much time and money was spent on producing this farcical document.' The columnist thought it was a 'nonsensical work', full of 'arrant nonsense' and 'typically committee-written crap'. He insisted that he was unreservedly for complete equality of opportunity, but that the authors were 'strident, complex-ridden harpies'.

Despite these defensive squeals, the NUJ went on to accept a code of practice which included a clause opposed to material which discriminates against women. Since then the issue has been debated in other unions and at the TUC women's conference. Clause 10 of the TUC *Charter for Women*, published in 1979 (see page 100) states: 'The content of journals and other union publications should be presented in non-sexist terms.'

In spite of this shift of opinion, *The Yorkshire Miner*, the newspaper for that region of the National Union of Mineworkers, started publishing nude pin-ups in 1981. Arthur Scargill's rather lame excuse was that the pin-ups helped to sell the paper. He met with strong opposition from women, who argued that the blatant use of pictures of nude women in a union newspaper made a mockery of TUC policies on equal opportunities. Unions couldn't have it both ways. They could not make statements about the need to end discrimination at the same time as condoning publications which degraded and trivialised women. But at least the issue was now out in the open, and sexism, a word barely heard of ten years ago, is now widely debated.

Sexual harassment

'Sexual harassment is a trade union issue', says a leaflet from the National and Local Government Officers Association (NALGO). 'We cannot hope for long-term success with our policies on equal opportunities in recruitment, promotion and training if women are seen simply as sex objects.' Sexual harassment has emerged as a serious problem, and one that can take many forms:

* men make it clear to women that they will not get promotion or a job unless they agree to give sexual favours.
* women become stressed or may be driven out of work by unwanted sexual advances or persistent touching.
* women are expected to tolerate sexual 'jokes' and offensive remarks.

Any woman may experience sexual harassment, whether she is young or old, a waitress, a clerk or a university lecturer. It is a particularly acute problem in offices where women work for a male boss. Many NALGO members are in this situation, and a survey of them in Liverpool found that 52 per cent of the women had experienced sexual harassment at work. In Canada, a government employees' union put the figure as high as 80 per cent.

NALGO activists argue that the only way to break through the private suffering and anger of thousands of women is to bring the problem out into the open and use the trade union to deal with it. Women who are sexually harassed are encouraged to tell their shop stewards or branch representatives. This is not always easy if the union official is male, or if the man in question is in the same union, but it is a start nonetheless. In the United States, women have been active on the issue for some time. Two waitresses in Oakland, for instance, took their case to court and were awarded $275,000 compensation for the sexual harassment they had suffered.

British unions are beginning to move on the issue as pressure from women builds up. NALGO has taken a useful lead, and the problem was debated at the women's conference of the TUC for the first time in 1982, when a motion from the NUJ called on the women's advisory committee to develop guidelines for investigating grievances and dealing with offenders.

Sexual harassment at work is another example of a 'personal' issue that women have turned into a demand for trade-union action. Like abortion and images of women, sexual harassment has been discussed at length in the women's movement, and was taken into the unions by fairly small groups of women who were active in both organisations. From this activist base, debates spread through trade-union networks. Women become aware of them through direct contact with the women's movement, or through women's events organised by their unions or the TUC. They then argue the points with their colleagues at work and raise them at their own branch meetings and union conferences.

Inevitably, the debates have made most headway in unions with a high proportion of female members and where there are well-established women's advisory committees to act as a focus for women's action. Unions with predominantly male memberships have been relatively untouched. So the success of campaigns at a national level does not necessarily indicate a change of attitudes to women in traditional areas of male manual work. But the struggles of women's politics *have* been well established in trade unionism. And the boundaries of union action have been extended as a result.

So women and unions need each other. Women need to combine with other workers to defend their interests and apply pressure for change. By so doing they strengthen and enrich the whole trade-union movement. Women are not the remedial class of the trade unions, in need of special treatment to bring them up to standard. Women make a vital contribution, both through their shared interests with men and through their distinctive traditions and concerns as women. There are, of course, still obstacles to women playing a full part in existing union structures. But to those who question the extent of women's activity in trade unions, one might pose the converse question: how actively are trade unions prepared to support women's struggles? Are there barriers that prevent men supporting women? These questions, and the underlying problem of what equality means, are taken up in Chapter 2.

Also, we must not forget that trade unionism depends on the energy and commitment of individuals. The portraits in Chapters 3 and 6 are the personal stories of four women activists, and give an insight into the problems they face and the achievements in which they take pride.

2.

Sisters and Brothers

The following conversation took place between four women on a shop stewards' course in 1981:

Sandra: Women are not as strong as the men, are they? I mean the men's unions have been going a lot longer than ours.

Tricia: But it's not a different union! It's not *men's* union, it's *our* union.

Nora: Yes, but they have a bigger hold on it, obviously, and they are trying to keep the women out. This is the problem, and you are having to fight twice as hard to get on, aren't you?

Tricia: Therefore we should make better shop stewards and officials when we get there, because we've had to fight twice as hard!

Sue: They started it, that's what they think.

Tricia: Well, they did, but they started it when men did the work and women stayed at home.

Sue: They think we are interfering.

Nora: It comes to the same thing. Men think women are inferior; they can't think, or they can't do anything, or . . .

Tricia: . . . or that you are a trouble-maker.

Nora: They just don't like to think that a woman knows more than they do. That's the top and bottom of it.

Tricia: Yes, it's male chauvinism again, isn't it?

The conversation reflects the women's experiences in their different unions and at work. Sandra, a member of the General and Municipal Workers Union (GMWU), worked in a toy factory for a tiny wage and was very new to trade unions. Nora felt aggrieved that her union had been slow to resist the loss of women's jobs in the paper products factory where she worked. Tricia was a skilled worker, a woman working among men, and Sue was struggling to find a foothold in NALGO.

How typical is their experience, particularly the feeling that unions are more to do with men than with women? Is it true that women in unions are ignored or under-valued? What about men's attitudes towards women? And how far have we established equality between men and women in the trade-union movement?

First of all, let's take a closer look at the notion of equality. Trade unions are, numerically, dominated by men, especially at the higher levels. This has meant that traditional ways of organising and bargaining have been shaped by men rather than women. Given this background, what is equality for women? Does it mean giving women the opportunity to learn to behave, think and act like men; to do their jobs, adopt their styles of leadership and learn their committee rules? This is surely a false equality. It requires that only women change. Men carry on the same, while women lose some of their femaleness. It results in the situation that Pam, a shop steward in a brewery, describes: 'I'm not seen as a woman in here; I'm just one of the lads.'

At the time, this may seem like an advance. But it is usually a temporary gain, a special place reserved for a particular individual who has 'made it' among the men. She is an exception, someone her male colleagues may well describe as 'Great, just like one of us', or 'Smashing—a real fighter, not like the other women.' It is a measure of her success in their eyes. The men may not change their attitudes to women as a result, and will expect each new woman to prove herself on their terms.

Real equality is something different. It is achieved through women having the space and flexibility to act as they choose, organise how they wish, and fight on the issues they think are important—without losing their identity as women and without a label saying 'second class'. It means being able to be powerful as a trade unionist *and* a woman. This is not a soft role, a modern version of flimsy femininity. It is a proud role that values the work women do and the things women achieve.

> We are not second-class citizens, we are vital. Well we are. (Celia, APEX)

> If you look in our factory we are two-thirds of the workforce keeping the place going, so we *must* be important. I mean, if only women would realise how important we are to industry. (June, APEX)

> I like frilly nighties the same as everyone else, but it doesn't mean you've got to sit there like a tin of prunes. Not that I *could* sit there like a tin of prunes anyway! (Celia)

Equality is not a simple thing to measure. We can start by looking at the statistics on women's membership of, and participation in, trade unions. But we need to go further than this. The experience of many women in unions is that they are still not getting the facilities and support they need. In this chapter we shall look at the reasons why this is the case.

Patterns of membership

In the years since the last war, women's membership of unions has shot up. In 1948, women made up less than one-fifth of trade union members. Now, one in three trade unionists is female. Without this influx of women, total trade union membership would have been almost static. In fact, it has grown from nine million in 1948 to twelve million in 1981.

Some unions have changed dramatically. NUPE, NALGO and the Confederation of Health Service Employees (COHSE) grew with the post-war expansion of local and national government and the formation of the National Health Service. Many of the new jobs were for women. Between 1968 and 1978, NUPE and COHSE almost tripled their female memberships, as nurses, dinner ladies and hospital workers flocked to join. White-collar jobs in the civil service and industry increased too. As a result, the number of women in the Civil and Public Services Association (CPSA) went up by half, and in APEX it doubled.

At the same time, many traditional areas of manual work declined. Men's jobs on the railways and in mining vanished rapidly. Women lost jobs in hosiery and textiles. Instead, they had to find jobs in the expanding service industries, or in white-collar areas. Indeed, in the period from 1948 to 1974 the number of jobs in health, education and local government more than doubled, and those in insurance, banking and finance increased by over 50 per cent.

The growth of women's employment and the growth of women's membership of trade unions went hand in hand. But the *proportion* of women workers in unions also increased. In 1948, only one in four working women was a trade union member. By 1980, the proportion had risen to two in five. Why did this happen? Partly because many of the new jobs were in large organisations, like local councils and multinational companies, where unions were generally recognised by the management. In some instances, there were already closed shops in operation which women joined as a condition of employment. The number of new jobs created in the traditionally hard to organise small workplaces was much smaller.

In addition, women's expectations changed throughout the sixties and seventies. More and more married women wanted to return to work. Equal pay became one of the big issues of the sixties, and women began to stand up for their rights in a more militant fashion. From 1968 onwards, a new wave of feminism washed over the United States and Europe, bringing with it a challenge to traditional assumptions about women's role. Trade unions, for all their faults, were the natural vehicle through which women could pursue their new demands at work. And, with an eye to the future, some unions realised they had to recruit women if they were to continue to expand. So they mounted recruitment campaigns and began to accommodate women's demands—at least as far as equal pay was concerned.

In the last thirty years, women have made great strides towards equality of trade union membership, particularly in white-collar work. But several problem areas remain, making the overall picture of women's union membership patchy.

Room for improvement

In spite of the surge of membership, the proportion of working women in unions is still lower than that of men. Does this mean women are less union-minded? Not necessarily. As the TUC stated in its evidence to the Donovan commission in 1966:

> Where men are well organised in a particular plant, generally women are too. The fact that the proportion of women in employment who belong to trade unions is only about half that of men is mainly to be accounted for by differences in their industrial and occupational distribution.

In other words, more women than men work in jobs which unions have always found hard to organise. Over half the women in manual jobs are cleaners, caterers, hairdressers and service workers. Their wages are set by wages councils or employers as often as by collective bargaining. Their workplaces may be small, so that the relationship with the employer lacks the formality and remoteness of a large company. And nearly 40 per cent of women are part-timers—and neither the law nor collective bargaining offer sufficient protection to part-time workers.

All these factors make life difficult for the would-be union organis-er. As a result, many workplaces remain unorganised. A cleaner in a small private company is unlikely to be in a union, whereas her sister in a hospital will probably be in NUPE. The lady who works three days a week in the corner shop may never have been approached by USDAW, the shop workers' union, though her full-time colleagues in Woolworth are likely to be union members.

There are difficulties in white-collar work, too. Although nearly all office workers in local government and the civil service are in unions, the proportion drops to 50 per cent in banking and insurance, and lower still for offices in private companies. Paternalistic or hostile managers, a lack of union traditions and small numbers all act as barriers to unionisation.

One large group of women is even worse off—homeworkers. Most of the quarter of a million homeworkers are women, doing every-thing from toy-making and jewellery to packing Christmas crackers. The work is frequently boring and repetitive, and sometimes hazar-dous. A further 130,000 women work at home as childminders. Their wages, as for all homeworkers, may still work out at less than £1 per hour.

For many years, unions ignored their plight. Because homework-ing involved employers contracting out certain jobs to women for tiny sums, workers in factories could see it as a threat to their own wages and conditions. But attitudes have started to change and some attempts have been made to bring homeworkers under union protec-tion.

The GMWU, for example, has established a homeworkers' branch in Devon for rural women making gloves. This is a start, though the difficulties are great. Homeworkers are socially isolated from one another and have a vulnerable individual relationship with the em-ployer. Homeworking contains all the problems of women's employ-ment writ large.

Up the hierarchies
It is well known that men rule OK at all levels of trade-union hierarchy. Equality for women is still a distant dream. Although women now outnumber men in several major unions, they become

suddenly invisible among the full-time officers and executive members. In USDAW, for instance, women make up 63 per cent of the membership, but only 19 per cent of the executive and 8 per cent of the full-time officials. In some unions the situation is even worse. The TGWU has the second largest female membership of all British unions—330,000 women. Because the union is so large this is just 16 per cent of the total. Yet there are no women at all on the TGWU's 39-person executive, and out of 600 full-time officials only 6 are women—a paltry 1 per cent. The GMWU is another major union with no women on its executive although a third of the members are female—an ironic situation as the National Federation of Women Workers amalgamated with the union in 1920 with high hopes of continuing its excellent representation of women.

Several unions have carried out surveys to fill in the picture of women's participation in more detail. NUPE, for example, now has more women members than any other union. It has taken positive steps to encourage women, and things are improving—at least at shop steward level. Now 42 per cent of NUPE shop stewards are women, compared with 28 per cent in 1974. But at the next level, only 19 per cent of the branch district committee chairpersons are women. On the divisional councils there are virtually no women apart from those in reserved women's seats.

NATFHE, the union for teachers in further and higher education, drew up statistics on women's participation in 1981. The pattern is interesting, and is probably typical of unions for professional workers. Women are significantly, but not drastically, under-represented among branch secretaries and on the national executive—14 per cent and 16 per cent respectively, against a female membership of 23 per cent. Where women lose out badly is on the standing committees which look after the different sectors of education. Only 10 per cent of the elected committee members are women, yet these are important bodies dealing with negotiating priorities. Worse still, the one and only female regional officer has 54 male colleagues.

So the Invisible Woman is alive and well and lives in many a trade union office in London. She can also be found haunting the long corridors of the TUC. The general council of the TUC has no women members apart from those in special reserved seats. At the annual congress—once described as a sea of bald heads and baggy suits—you have to search quite hard for a female face. Only 112 out of the 1,200 delegates in 1979 were women. And the TUC makes sexist 'mistakes', such as sending out invitations to 'delegates and their wives'. Yet the TUC is a vital policy-making body for the whole movement. Resolutions passed at congress have been important in campaigns for equal pay, maternity rights and abortion. But the responsibility for carrying these issues into the TUC has fallen onto a very small number of women.

So the bare statistics show a considerable lack of equality between men and women in union structures. They boil down to the fact that large numbers of women have decisions made for them by men. In a male-dominated movement, this all too easily means that women's interests are lost. The important question to ask now is why this situation still exists.

What holds women back?

When NUPE asked its branch district committees why women's occupations were under-represented on their committees, the (pre-dominantly male) secretaries replied as follows: 30 per cent blamed women's apathy or lack of trade union-mindedness, 24 per cent said absence of stewards, 14 per cent said women were reluctant to become stewards, and 9 per cent mentioned travel problems. When *women* in NUPE were asked on a shop stewards' course what held them back they came up with 11 very different reasons. The two sets of replies are shown in the following table and show how differently men and women view women in the union.

Some of the issues in the table have been discussed for some time—the problems of domestic commitments and meeting times, for example. But the points about male attitudes and women feeling intimidated have generally been swept under the carpet. Are they too dangerous? Will men be upset? They are real barriers to equality and need to be brought out into the open. It is important to listen to what women have to say about their own experiences. Most of the quotes below are taken from women on shop stewards' courses and give some personal views of the difficulties pin-pointed by the NUPE women.

Why are women under-represented in NUPE?

Answers given by women shop stewards	*Answers given by branch district committee secretaries*
Meeting structure is formal and confusing.	Apathy.
	Lack of union-mindedness.

Meetings at difficult times, often in pubs.

Male union reps don't understand women's problems.

Union doesn't take up women's issues in negotiations.

Full-time officers don't see women's problems as important and serious.

National negotiations make the union seem remote.

Problems due to type of work—women are often part-timers.

Women have heavy domestic commitments.

Women lack confidence.

Women are intimidated on courses.

Women are afraid to become active because of threats of intimidation by employers.

Absence of stewards.

Women reluctant to be stewards.

Travel problems.

'Meetings at difficult times'

Today some women are lucky enough to be able to say:

> It used to be a man's world, but it isn't now, is it? A few years ago you did what your husband said; now you say what *you* want. (Julie, TGWU)

Even if women now speak out more and husbands are better at helping in the house, it is still women who carry the greatest burden of housework and childcare. This is a barrier to trade-union activity. Time is short, fatigue is common, and getting to meetings in the evening is difficult.

> I already do two jobs—I'm a worker and a mother. Now you are saying I should do three jobs and be a shop steward as well? (June, AUEW)

> If a man wants to go out he just goes. If a woman wants to go out

she has to ask or make arrangements for the kids and that. It's a lot more difficult. (Avril, AUEW)

I get home, turn around to my husband and say, 'I've got a branch meeting at seven o'clock so I must be away prompt because I'm shop steward and I'm expected to be there. Tea is in the oven, the kids' jamas is ready. Have them in bed by half seven.' He says, 'Fair enough, but be back by nine o'clock because I'm going down the club for a game of dominoes'. To go to the branch meeting you've got to have everything ready in advance so you can more or less run in, get changed, get ready, and that's it—you're away. (Shirley, TGWU)

To get to a union residential course Janice, a shop steward, prepared five days' meals in advance and left them in the fridge with labels saying 'Monday tea', 'Tuesday lunch' etc. One evening she was told her husband had rung and would she phone home urgently. Terrified that something had happened to her child she phoned, only to hear her husband ask, 'How long do I cook the shepherds pie for?' More seriously, a woman on a NUPE course couldn't hide the bruises on her arms where her husband had beaten her for going on the course. She had had the courage to come—how many women stay away?

Many union meetings are held in pubs and clubs. As well as finding transport difficult, many women dislike the atmosphere of beer and smoke. Others are wary of travelling alone to and from pubs at night. And in the north of England there can be the problem of having to be signed into a club by a man—something hardly likely to help women feel equal in the union!

But changes can be made. On page 36 Ellen describes how lively and well-attended her branch is. NUPE is now encouraging sub-branches of informal meetings where groups of women can meet and discuss their work. Branches can do a number of things to help women become more involved:

   * Holding meetings in working time. Lunchtimes may not be good enough—they are needed for shopping. Unions need to negotiate time off so that members can attend without loss of wages.

   * Holding meetings in a place that is easy to get to, and where women feel comfortable.

   * Making creche facilities available or, if this is not possible, paying baby-sitting expenses.

   * Breaking down the formality of meetings and encouraging open discussion.

'Male union reps don't understand . . .'
Even when they get to meetings, women often experience difficulties,
this time in the attitudes of the men.

> When I'm with men I don't have as much to say as when there is
> all women, because I don't want to be ridiculed by a man. They
> tend to make fun of you. I've noticed it. It's wrong, but it's still
> the attitude. (Angie, TGWU)

> Often the men in charge don't listen to what the women have got
> to say. They don't think the women have got anything worth
> talking about, and that attitude keeps a lot of women down.
> (Trish, AUEW)

> Your ideas tend to be tolerated but not listened to. Talking in a
> group the serious remarks tend to be addressed to the men. (Liz,
> TGWU)

Trade-union women are not alone in this experience of being
talked over by men. In her book *Man Made Language*, Dale Spender describes how men dominate conversations. Men interrupt
women but it is hard for women to interrupt men. Men define the
topic under discussion while women play a secondary role by asking
questions. She taped many conversations, including a workshop on
sexism and education in London. Although there were 32 women
and only 5 men there, the men talked for over half the time. They
also continually pulled the discussion back to what *they* wanted to
talk about. This is a familiar experience to women in union meetings.

The problem can be compounded where women are in a small
minority and when a lot of jargon is used.

> I was at a meeting with the management about repairs to the
> building, and I was the only women there. When I came out the
> senior staff rep said 'You're supposed to say something!' and I
> was thinking, 'I'm not going to say anything, I was the only
> woman there'. There wasn't any woman on the management
> side either, so I just sat and said nothing. (Celia, APEX)

> We've found that when you're sitting at some of these meetings
> you tend to sit in the background and they are talking way above
> your head. You think, 'Well, I'm going to look a right twit here
> if I don't know what I'm talking about'. You're not absolutely
> ignorant, but half the time you feel as if you are. (Pat, APEX)

Male attitudes in unions reflect those in society, so men commonly make sexist assumptions about women's role. This can make women feel unwelcome or out of place in a union. It re-inforces the feeling that the union is for men.

> A lot of women feel that the union is still predominantly a man's world, and that it takes a very strong-willed woman to encroach on this world. (Bev, APEX)

> Male trade unionists are often at best condescending and unhelpful and at worst hostile and anti-women. I accept that there are some good men! But sometimes the men who you expect to be supportive because they are socialist are also patronising or uninterested in women's issues. (Cathy, NALGO)

> My husband is in the union, but he hates me being active. He calls me the shop-stupid. (May, AUEW)

> My convener's always going on about equal rights. The other day he said to me, 'What more do you want, you've got equal rights already'. But I've heard him say that he'd have no intention of ever cooking the dinner. That's his wife's job and the kitchen is no place for him. (Nora, AUEW)

Similar feelings were voiced by women in a tobacco factory in Bristol which Anna Pollert describes in *Girls, Wives, Factory Lives*. To the workers, the union was just another 'them'. Their lack of involvement was due to more than domestic commitments. Becoming active would have meant breaking the boundaries between men's and women's worlds—something that was very hard to do, even for women who were conscious of a need for changes at work. Pressures from home forced the women to accept, however grudgingly, a sexual division of interests where the men were 'the union' and they just 'let things slide' or 'didn't bother'. As Anna Pollert puts it:

> Whatever women desired or intended to do, both practical and ideological obstacles were placed before them by a ruling ideology and the very husbands who, in another context, condemned women as 'bad trade unionists'.

Sometimes women escape the problem. In spite of difficulties, some activists like Harriet (see page 86) say they wouldn't have achieved as much as they did without the support of men. Here is another woman whose experience has been good:

> Well, where I work there is more men, but I still have my say. They listen to what I say and are very good at helping me. (Mary, AUEW)

But sexism is very subtle. It can be hard to pin down. It is often there in the language or style of a discussion, making women feel uncomfortable, diffident and self-conscious. It is reflected in the way men sit, limbs stretched out, filling the available space, while women curl up, legs twined round each other, slightly huddled. It is in the unspoken assumptions of what unions are really about and the hard, masculine image of the militant. It is about a woman feeling that she does not exist when the talk is of dear brothers, the lads, a man's wage and Mr Chairman. It can be in things as simple as the arrangement of a room and the way introductions are made. All these convey the persistent message to women—the message that to be male is normal, real and important, and to be female is to be different and less important.

Perhaps the best way to illustrate this is to use an example. The following account is of a meeting which went badly wrong for women, but which many men might think was perfectly normal:

> It is the first meeting of the regional women's advisory committee of a major union. The room is large and formal with a U-shaped board table. The women come in, get each other cups of coffee and sit close together at one end of the table, chatting and making introductions. Their ages range from 25 to 50. Three male officers sit looking uncomfortable at the other end of the table.

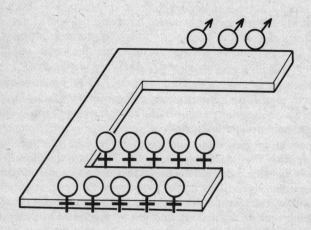

The regional secretary of the union flounces in, winking at the women. 'So nice to see so many girls here.' He sits himself at the top of the table. 'Right now, you're far too crowded over there—half of you move over.' 'We're OK here.' 'No, no, we must do things properly. This is a sub-committee of the regional council, you know.' The women move so the room now looks like this:

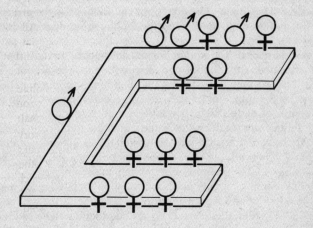

He then monologues for ten minutes. 'Just to get you started . . . conference decision to get more women involved . . . must have officers here to make sure you know regional policy . . . committee must be properly constituted . . . ' The women look attentive but unimpressed. 'Need the men be here? What about if we want to talk about, er, delicate matters?' 'Oh come, come, I'm a family man myself you know, and we can't go against the rules. Now I've got important business to attend to, so I suggest you elect yourselves a chairman—or should I say chairperson?—and you can get on with your meeting.'

One woman is duly elected and takes the regional secretary's seat as he flourishes out of the room with more winks and a wave. The women are now physically separated from each other—quite different from the way they sat when they first came in. One of them has been put in authority over the others and has to sit on a raised seat at the head of the table. Everyone has to speak loudly to be heard, and must obey procedural rules. Male officials are watching to make sure they don't step outside existing policy. Minutes are taken by one of the men—the same official that had drawn up the agenda.

Afterwards, two of the women say how they feel. The meeting had been a start, but they didn't feel very happy with it as a women's advisory committee. They didn't like the officials interrupting. They hadn't had much of a chance to get to know each other and were not quite sure what the committee was supposed to be for.

What went wrong? The women wanted an informal, friendly meeting to exchange experiences and discuss common problems—as women. Instead they were forced into a formal committee. Their discussion was crushed under rules and procedures, and inhibited by the presence of the officials. It was clear that they could only plan activities which would not challenge the regional secretary or regional policy, so the very things the women wanted to talk about—negotiating priorities, policies, attitudes—were blocked from the start. And this was supposed to encourage more women to get involved!

Any one aspect of sexism may seem small in itself—the language someone uses, the seating arrangements, the time of the meeting. But added together these make up an enormous weight of male traditions and attitudes that women have to cope with day after day, hour after hour. It is little wonder that many women feel discouraged and unconfident, fearing that they fail as trade unionists because they don't act as men appear to do.

This is a challenge to men. Equality for women would mean men giving up some of their traditions, some of their power and authority. It will not be easy for them to share control. If they fail to change, they trap women into a false equality by saying, 'Be like us, or stay in second place'. If they can learn to appreciate women's value and to take women's interests seriously, the results may not be as threatening as many men fear. Both men and women stand to gain from unions that are less bureaucratic and more in touch with the membership. And as the ACTT publication, *Patterns of Discrimination*, says:

> The more areas of working life the union is involved in, the stronger it will be . . . It will mean that more members feel they have a contribution to make to the union—and that the union has a contribution to make to them.

'The union seems remote'

If you ask someone to describe the average trade unionist, they will probably talk about militant car workers, railwaymen or miners. They will rarely mention cleaners, sewing machinists or nurses. Trade unions have a highly masculine image in the public mind. Men in overalls, men shouting on picket lines, men in suits talking on the television, miners with blackened faces. This is partly a contemporary image constructed by banner headlines in the press: DOCKERS SAY NO, and BL MEN THREATEN TO STRIKE. It also has a historical basis, as people look back to the mythical old days when men were real men and the dole queues were all blokes in caps.

Women are invisible in this image. Few women work in the industries with the highest strike records—cars, mining, steel, shipbuilding and the docks. Struggles in smaller workplaces and in the caring professions make less attractive news stories to the conflict-hungry media (unless, of course, patients are suffering). Women's absence from national negotiations means that it is always a man who comments on the latest round of talks, even if they concern teachers or nurses.

There are two assumptions behind the image. There is the idea that what men do is 'real' trade unionism. Also, many people think that militant action is the most important sign of a strong trade union. Both these assumptions conceal women's interests and the value of women's activity.

a) 'Real' trade unionism   When a group of academics from Warwick University carried out a survey of NUPE stewards in 1974, they found slightly different patterns of activity for men and women. Women were less active in what they called the 'real business' of trade unionism—representation and collective bargaining. But they questioned the validity of their own findings. Perhaps, they suggested, the popular view of how a good shop steward should act was simply a trade union version of the stereotype of the dominant male. Hence men conform more easily than women to people's expectations of an active trade unionist.

Could this be true? Male and female shop stewards undoubtedly have a lot in common. They face many of the same problems as workers and trade unionists. But there *are* some important differences. There is still a considerable degree of separation between men's work and women's work, and where the work is different both priorities and methods of organising are bound to differ too. Do women also approach problems differently? The experience of the women's movement suggests that women *do* organise differently from men if they have the chance to do so.

Let's take bargaining as an example. Collective bargaining involves a union team and a management team sitting round a table and working through proposals, offers and threats until a compromise solution is hammered out. Only exceptionally does the bargaining process break down and industrial action take place. Bargaining is a game. It has unwritten rules and well-tried tactics. Both sides run courses to train their people in bargaining techniques. At present, the majority of national (and local) negotiators are men. As personnel management has taken over responsibility for industrial relations in most organisations, personnel work has ceased to be a mainly female area and has become a profession dominated by men. On the union side, John Torode parodied the way union officials feel about bargaining when he wrote about pay talks at British Leyland in the *Guardian*, 29 October, 1981:

> Negotiating makes you feel good. It makes you feel ten feet tall . . . The team troops into the smoke-filled room. They to-and-fro across a table as equals with senior managers. They receive phone calls late at night between rounds of talks to see if something can't be fixed. There are cameras and mikes to be thrust aside with self-important growls of 'no comment' . . .
>
> The whole business is a tribal ritual which confirms the import-ance of the activist and massages his conscience. Through his effort the wage offer has been forced up and the lot of the lads has been improved.

Can you visualise women here? Even if women felt the same way, which is doubtful, it would in any case be impossible for many wives and mothers to be available at all hours of the day and night. Most men can only achieve this through the support of their wives at home. Notice also the casual use of 'he' and 'the lads'. The whole piece has an intensely masculine feel to it.

What if women do not *want* to participate in all this? Perhaps they are right and it is the traditions, not women, that must change. This is not to say negotiations are not important. They are. But if more women were involved, the accepted pattern might change. At the moment, there are too few women at a national level to see what impact they might have, and we do not know how much of the style is dictated by the management. But there are already successful female negotiators in some factories and offices, and experience suggests they tend to adopt a more direct and informal style with less game-playing and fewer lengthy sessions.

We return again to the idea that women must shape trade-union activity to suit their own needs. The price of their involvement must not be the uncritical adoption of established methods. Women could transform some of these traditions, and make the trade-union movement, as a whole, all the stronger.

b) A question of militancy The association between trade union-ism and militancy poses problems for women. When accused of being less militant than men, women activists will point to many significant strikes led by women, from the matchgirls in the last century to Grunwicks and Lee Jeans. Militancy has been growing among white-collar workers too. Civil servants and social workers, typists and clerks have all shown a willingness to take industrial action. Bitter-ness about low pay has motivated women to strike on many occa-sions. Mary O'Gorman, a school auxiliary, described her feelings about being out on strike in 1979:

> I'd go on strike again, to get more money I would. I'd get a better paid job if I could, but there is no job, only this one, which will fit in. I like to be in when my youngest gets in and my husband, who's disabled, needs lots of things done for him. Now, after rent, we've £25 a week left for the three of us, for everything. So it's not asking a lot, we're just asking not to have to scrape from day to day. (*SR* 80)

But the question of women's militancy cannot be divorced from the jobs women do. Many women's jobs lack the economic power that makes a strike effective. While women in production jobs can use the strike weapon as effectively as men, cleaners and filing clerks lack their power to disrupt the employer's business. For women in caring jobs there is a further problem. If home helps and attendants in old people's homes go on strike, the dependent elderly are likely to suffer more than the employer. And relationships can be impossibly difficult when the women return to work. So a nurse or a teacher trying to decide whether or not to strike has far more to consider than the loss of her wages. She may be in an acute dilemma about the right thing to do—a dilemma which arises not from weakness or lack of solidarity but from her genuine concern about those in her care.

Moreover, many women do not wish to identify with the media image of strikers as tough men on agressive picket lines. So the fact that women service workers *do* strike shows how strongly they feel about certain issues. As Sharon Campbell, a student nurse and COHSE shop steward, put it:

> The point is, when people say, "How can you strike and leave patients at risk?" we must reply, "How can Mr Ennals [then Minister of Health] close nurseries, day-centres for old people, family planning clinics and whole hospitals up and down the country . . . putting hundreds of lives at risk, many on the dole, *and* making more work for the women who end up looking after the young, the old and the sick—*unpaid*?" (*WV* 26)

When it comes to the crunch, women have always been prepared to take strong determined action. The vote, birth control and equal pay were not handed to women on a plate. Women had to fight for them, and did so with energy and strength. They developed an imaginative variety of methods too. Colourful demonstrations, streetcorner meetings, songs and parliamentary protests have all been used to good effect.

So the feelings that deter women from union activity—like the NUPE women's fear that the union does not take their interests seriously—are not simply based on superficial attitudes. Sexism is a powerful force. Entrenched thinking about the real business of trade unions means that women's action is only recognised when it fits into traditional patterns. This it does only to a degree. Women's distinctive interests are too often concealed under the tough, masculine image of trade unions.

It is not very helpful if the only concept of equality held up to women is to learn how to conform to this image. Genuine equality in trade unions is still a long way off—equality based on an understanding that variation exists and individuals differ, but that each person, female or male, is valuable in their own right. This will be difficult to achieve, but it is surely worth fighting for.

The NUPE shop stewards identified two other factors which hold women back. These were women's heavy domestic commitments and the problems of the type of work women do, particularly part-time work. These areas are so important that they deserve a chapter to themselves (see Chapter 4).

3.

Portraits

Ellen Parker: 'Mum's having one of her union fits again'

Ellen Parker works as a clerk for the Prudential Insurance Company in Consett, County Durham—a town still reeling from the closure of the steelworks in 1980. Ellen was one of many local people in the Save Consett Campaign. She is a branch secretary in the National Union of Insurance Workers, a small white-collar union for employees of large insurance companies. She is 43, married, and has three children aged from 17 to 22.

Ellen's union involvement started five years ago. Her grade, known as district managers' clerks, consists entirely of women. Every year the women in the north east of England got together for a day out.

'I got involved on a train trip from Newcastle to Edinburgh. On the train we were discussing our own grade and how poorly paid we were. As we have no communication with each other we loved these get-togethers and felt it would be far better if we could have done it more frequently. We had no official union representation apart from the national executive negotiating for us centrally, so we decided to ask whether we could form a branch for the clerks. That's entirely women—not because the job isn't open to men. It's just that no-one has ever applied because the rates of pay are so low.'

The idea of forming a branch of their own caught on, and an inaugural meeting was called in Newcastle. 'At first we were told there wouldn't be enough people interested to form a branch, but we had to take over a whole hotel suite, so many turned up! The divisional rep. couldn't understand where they had all come from, but I think the trips we organised made people realise there were clerks in exactly the same offices with exactly the same problems, and they were keen to discuss their problems with each other. The only way you could do this was by forming a branch, which we did without any difficulty.'

Ellen took on the job of branch secretary. A friend, Elsie, became branch chairperson and is now the national secretary for their grade. From that meeting, the branch went from strength to strength. Meetings are held bi-monthly in Newcastle and are very well attended—a remarkable achievement as the members are scattered from Darlington to Berwick-on-Tweed. And two thirds of the eighty or so members are part-timers. 'About thirty-five to forty-five come to meetings. The girls are very verbal and very interested. There's no difficulty getting people to meetings.'

Members get time off from work to attend, so meetings are held on weekdays. 'We start at ten and finish at four, and we try and put a lot of interest into it. We try and make it a personal discussion, but we never shirk telling them how deeply trying a problem is, and we try and make sure everyone is warned in advance if there's going to be any changes in district offices.' In the afternoons they often have guest speakers 'so there's someone interesting to talk to'.

Another unusual feature of the branch is its social programme. The women have been to the theatre and have organised Christmas shopping trips to London. There was even a weekend holiday in Norway! Ellen feels the social activities are important because they help to foster a sense of togetherness: 'It has formed relationships that would never, never have been formed. There is a camaraderie that is absolutely fantastic. And I think the social activities often lead to items coming to us as union members. If you are talking to a girl and she says what has been happening in her office, you can say, "Well, that should be told, we should know about that, it is an incorrect practice and we'll stop that".'

Ellen praises her members for their willingness to protect each other and back up the branch officials. The one exception was their refusal to vote for a closed shop—something which Ellen favours. 'They will not have anything to do with a closed shop, and that was the only time I felt as if I'd been sort of slapped in the face.'

So what motivated her to become branch secretary? 'Well, first of all I felt that my pay was inadequate. We did our own survey of jobs—clerical grades, the civil service and so on—and we found we were below the lowest paid in these situations. We felt, OK, it was a good company to work for, it looks after its workers, but you still need that representation at the top to push for equal pay and for better conditions all round. I honestly think no-one knew about the work we did. We cover a multitude of duties, from answering the telephone and serving at the counter to being your district manager's personal assistant—and we get very little training.'

She had 'no conception of union activities, none whatsoever'. But she was politically active as a member of the Labour Party. 'It was a difficult step into trade unionism because I had to decide which was the most important to me. I felt I had a strong role to play in the union because there are very few women who will actually say they will devote their free time to the care and help of other people in the company sphere. You have to have the support of your husband and family to enable you to do that. There are so many calls on your time.'

Because Ellen lives close to the office where she works she often pops back in the evenings to do her union business. It can be difficult to fit this in with the family. 'I often have to put them out because I rely on the children to put the dinner on. Or if I go away to a divisional meeting I'm away for a couple of days and I have to rely on them, you know—letting the house tick over and looking after their father. Luckily they are all grown up, but it is still an inconvenience for them.'

'Sometimes I get very up-tight about something I feel very strongly about. You often hear this quote that women should get back to the kitchen sink, and this really aggravates me. In that type of situation I tend to get very domineering at home. They just let me get on with it now. They just say, "Mum's having one of her union fits again!" '

Within the union, Ellen's grade has had to battle for attention. Most of the union officers are men as they have been drawn from the ranks of the insurance officers rather than the clerks.

'At first I think the men were shy of the women being involved. I think they were unsure of how women would react to their sort of male environment. We were very much left out in the cold—you would walk into a room and everyone would stop talking. They would put up barriers by saying, "Oh, you don't want to come to conference, it's all men" or "It wouldn't be any good for you, you don't understand it anyway". But once we had started to get to our feet and debate, I think this was when the change of attitude started to become noticeable. The men started to listen to what we had to say, because we always tried to be very clear and precise, and very verbal. They accept us now.

'I don't think there's a single workplace or meeting I've ever been to where I didn't find men who were chauvinistic bcause it suited their purpose. It is a veil to hide their true feelings really, possibly wishing to hide their own inadequacies. Because women have to be good. If you are going to be in the trade union movement you have to be fantastic. If you just bumble your way through you will never do anything for the women. But I have never let a male chauvinist person rile me. As a young person they did, but I am far too old now to be riled by any man!'

She sees considerable change in herself from the shy, retiring person she thought she was. 'I was a very quiet person. I wouldn't say boo to a goose. At the beginning my knees used to knock, and I am one of these people who flush easily.'

'The first year at conference I was absolutely sick with fright, and I just couldn't cope with it. I entered the hall and there was just this sea of faces, and it was a traumatic experience for me, you know, just to go and sit down at a long table with people I'd never met before in my life. That was my first conference, and after that I felt I had something to give and I wanted to participate. It changed me from the kind of person that would accept anybody's decision to the other type of person that won't accept poor service, that won't accept shoddy goods, and won't accept that women are second-class citizens.'

One step along the way was to enrol on a TUC shop stewards' course, mainly because she wanted to improve her public speaking so that she would feel less afraid in meetings where she was the only woman. She went on to advanced courses, and is a great believer in adult education. 'You have got to realise that you are an important person, as important as the next person, or man. Once you have learned that you are not an idiot, you know, that you are not just capable of washing dishes and ironing shirts, then you can have your own personal objective.'

For herself, she would like to see her grade 'stand on its own as a grade, with the qualifications, the pay and all the little fringe benefits it actually should have. I would like to see women equal with the men, with a chance to become executives.' To help achieve this, both Ellen and Elsie have ambitions to gain seats on the national executive of the union.

'I would like to change the attitude my union has to women. I would want them to see that women are capable of becoming very high executives in the union, and that we are able to negotiate with management. We are never given that sort of chance. We sit on various committees but never the top jobs in the union. I am sure that the time will come that from somewhere in our grade we are going to get presidents of the union.'

She knows there is a lot to learn from the experienced men, but also feels that 'it is very difficult for most men to see the caring side of life. I don't think they have this softness about them. I don't mean softness as a push-over, I think . . . merciful, that is what I would say. Caring is something that all unions should do. The fact that you are in a big union shouldn't take away from the fact that each individual member is important to that union. That is how it seems to me. If more women were involved they may bring out this personal side of it.'

Ellen is an activist who looks strongly to the future, and who has clear ideas about what she hopes to achieve for her members. How does she feel looking back on the five years since the branch was formed? 'Well, I'm proud that the men do treat us as equals within the union now. I'm just proud to be a trade unionist and I would advocate trade unionism no matter where I went. I still say that people who bash the trade union movement don't look at life and don't look at what has happened in the past. They don't read their history books. They don't realise that what they have today is solely because of the trade union movement—and that is what I am proud of.'

Lillian Dunwoodie: 'You have to care about people'

Lillian Dunwoodie is a cleaner in a hospital on Tyneside. She has been a NUPE shop steward for a year, representing ancillary staff. When this interview took place she had just been elected secretary of her branch—a busy, large branch covering five hospitals and a number of clinics.

When she started as a cleaner eleven years ago Lillian joined the union straight away. 'When you come in, you want to be in a union because you need protection. I had worked in a factory before and I realised the unions are a good thing. You must have something behind you. It is a good insurance.'

During the so-called winter of discontent the cleaner's shop steward left the union. No-one offered to take over the job. Soon afterwards, the branch secretary called a meeting for ancillary staff. Lillian went along in a somewhat unusual guise and emerged as the new shop steward.

'I like to laugh, I like to make people laugh, you know. When this meeting came up my daughter was going to a fancy dress party, so I borrowed her Miss Piggy mask. I went into the committee room, which is one of the poshest rooms in the hospital, got into the biggest chair and sat with this Miss Piggy mask on. I was absolutely cooked underneath it and everyone was hee-hawing with laughter. Jonothan [the full-time official] and the branch secretary came in, and Jonothan looked at us as if to say, "Well, she's a nut!" '

As the meeting started Lillian discarded the mask and spoke against cuts in the cleaning staff. When it came to nominations for shop steward, someone called out, 'Lillian Dunwoodie—she's always a good talker'.

'Someone else said "I second that" and someone daft said "I third it". So I was very, very embarrassed, I must say. I said, "Oh no, I can't do it", knowing nothing about it at all. The only thing I knew about unions was that they were there for protection—a very essential thing—but I had no idea how they ran or anything.'

After some encouragement from the official Lillian said she would try it. 'I thought, "Well, it's a challenge, it's something different". You can vegetate a little bit in a job like this. It becomes monotonous, because each day you know that at one o'clock you'll be serving teas out, at three o'clock you'll be serving teas out, at dinner time you'll be washing dishes, and you can time each job you'll be doing.

'I felt very strongly about things. I'm always one that if I think I'm right I'll fight to . . . against King and country, you know. So I must have had the makings years ago but I never even gave it a thought.'

Both Lillian's children had married and left home recently which left a big gap in her home life. 'I really missed those children, really missed them. The bottom just fell out of my world. I've got a big house and I just rattle around in it. Tommy, my husband, is on night shift so I just used to read, watch telly, visit friends. So actually it was a challenge because I didn't think I could do it and it was something to get my teeth into.'

It might have been more difficult if the children had been small. 'When they were younger I devoted a lot of time to the children. They were never left with anyone. I mean when I wasn't there, Tommy was. This was why he went onto night shift actually. He could come off now, but he's been so used to it. He's been on night shift for 14 years, just so that he was in the house when I wasn't there. So perhaps Thursday night coming to branch meeting might have been a bit of a tie. But no, I think perhaps I could have done it long before I did. It was just I shied away from it.'

Lillian is shop steward for 35 members. All of them are women doing cleaning work around the hospital. About half are part-timers, and their wages are important. 'Women go out to earn a living. No woman in this hospital works for pin-money. I don't think there's a woman here that would let anyone say that to her. Most probably if it was said in a joke they would say, "Oh yes, I spend it all on fur coats", knowing fine well that it goes into the housekeeping.'

As a shop steward her job is to listen to the members and help sort out complaints. She feels it is very important to encourage the members to become more interested in the union.

'What I would like to do is to bring them together more to discuss things. Most of the women are married women with children so they can't come back after work. When they leave here they have shopping to do, they go home and cook meals, wash and get ready for the children coming home. Bringing them back at night is difficult and I would like to set up maybe a monthly meeting where we could get together for perhaps half an hour. We really need to get together a lot more to discuss things.'

As NUPE does not have a closed shop in the hospital there is a constant need to recruit new members. This often means battling against people's negative image of trade unions.

'They think whenever you are talking about unions you are talking about strikes. The two words seem to go together. They say, "Militant union—strikes". It's because of what they read in the newspapers, and a lot of people think what they read in the newspapers is right and correct. Basically, it is not about strikes, and that is what I want to get over to them. They are the union—we are not the union. If we said, "Go on strike", and they didn't want to, then they wouldn't go on strike because it is the members who vote for whatever they do.' Lillian prefers to see the union as a form of protection. 'You have someone to fight for you, to stand up for you if you are being victimised.'

Since she became shop steward a number of issues have cropped up. Under-staffing is a persistent problem. Her first meeting with the management on this stands out clearly in her memory. 'It was like going to the dentist the first time I went into the office. I had worked here for eleven years but I had never been into the office for anything so it was something new for me. So I went in and told her exactly what the girls felt. There were various things ranging from dodgy kettles to a staff shortage and girls feeling they were being picked on. I put it all down on this paper and read it all out bit by bit, shaking all the time. She said, "Oh well, Mrs Dunwoodie, we'll see what we can do".'

Eventually, after a joint meeting with COHSE and pressure from both unions, management made some improvements. They agreed to bring in extra staff and made plans for a 'bank' of cleaners who could be called in during holiday periods and sickness absence.

Lillian is also very concerned about jobs for young people. They should, she feels, have real jobs rather than temporary work on job creation schemes. 'I know a girl in an office where they said, "The yop will do it, hey yop go and get us a sandwich to have with our cup of tea". And this was dreadful, to me it was terrible. We had a young fellow here on one of these youth opportunity things, and I said, "How do you feel, Joe, when you draw your £16 odd and they are drawing their £70 and £80?". And he put his head down and said, "Ashamed". "Oh", I says, "Son, don't *ever* feel ashamed. It's us that should feel ashamed, offering you this. If you're doing a good job of work and you are getting a quarter of what you are entitled to, don't feel ashamed. Feel angry, but don't feel ashamed." '

Since becoming shop steward, Lillian has noticed her confidence increasing. She finds she can speak at meetings more easily than she expected, and now has a clearer idea of the shop steward's role.

'I'm trying now to get another girl in as shop steward. She said, "Oh, I don't know percentages", so I said, "Don't be daft, neither do I". Then she said, "Well, I'm not intelligent", and I says, "Phew, that rules me out as well". You have to basically care about people, and listen to their points. If you think they are being pushed down or anything then you step in. You don't have to be so intelligent. You don't need A levels for it, certainly not.

'But I have found I am more intelligent than I thought I was. This is a laugh too—I always used to read Catherine Cookson and things like that. Now all I read is NUPE stuff!'

A course for shop stewards, held in the NUPE offices in Newcastle, helped her through the early months. 'On the first day everyone was a bit nervous, but if you made a mistake it didn't matter. Everyone was so pleasant it was easy to talk, and all the tutors up there were very nice. I think we felt a bit pampered because we were in this nice room, plus having tea brought into us instead of serving other people's teas, you know.'

But she is critical of union jargon, finding that it needs a lot of effort to work out abbreviations and references to bits of the union structure. From the point of view of a shop steward the union beyond the branch level seems remote. Lillian sees her role as a very local one—it is other people's job to deal with higher levels of the union.

She explains this with reference to the course: 'That course was very good. It gave us the information we needed. But I felt we wouldn't need some of the stuff they were teaching us—when you would go to this council and that council, going higher and higher up the ladder. I would have thought it would have stopped short of that. Obviously by the time that was needed the full-time official would be taking over from a shop steward.'

In the same way she has, as yet, little experience of the role of the union's national executive or of the special women's seats.

'Well, where there's women going ahead and taking over a man's world I think it is a great idea, but I don't really know much about it, only the little things they touched on up at the course. As I say, once it started going up to executive level we were sort of lost off because we preferred to know the parts that were relevant to us. I just know that they are trying to get more women's seats, and I think it is a darned good idea because in this area of work there is more women than men.'

As branch secretary she will have more contact with the union structure. How does she feel about her new role, and does she plan to go any further?

'First of all when it came up I said it wasn't the sort of job I could take on as I haven't got the brains for it. Jonothan really encouraged me so I said I would give it a try. But I haven't thought about anything further on. No, obviously if I could I would, because I am very interested in it, but I think you have to have . . . I just want to do my best and see how I do the job, and then perhaps I might start to become ambitious.'

In one sense she was delighted to be nominated for branch secretary. 'How can I sound humble and proud together? I feel very proud that they've picked a branch secretary from the ancillary staff. Not for myself, I don't feel proud for myself—I feel apprehensive actually. I don't want to let anyone down.'

Her main aim is to get people together more and to make them feel that 'It is their union, not our union'. To do this she would like more time off from her cleaning job to visit other hospitals and get to know the shop stewards and members there. As she only works four days a week it will be difficult to find time for all the things she wants to do and not lose touch with her original members. But she has plenty of energy and optimism.

'I don't want to go away from the girls I work with. I want to be one of them as well. I won't drop out from being a shop steward because it is a very worthwhile job and a very enjoyable job.'

4.

Of Dinners to Bake and Clothes to Make

So the truth began to dawn then how I keep him fit and trim
So the boss can make a nice fat profit out of me and him,
And as a solid union man he got in quite a rage
To think that we're both working hard and getting one man's
    wage,
I said 'And what about the part-time packing job I do?
That's three men that I work for, love, my boss, your boss, and
    you!'

He looked a little sheepish and he said 'As from today,
The lads and me will see what we can do on equal pay.
Would you like a housewives' union? Do you think you should be
    paid
As a cook and as a cleaner, as a nurse and as a maid?'
I said 'Don't jump the gun, love, if you did your share at home,
Perhaps I'd have some time to fight some battles of my own!'

These verses from Sandra Kerr's song *The Maintenance Engineer*
beautifully describe a woman beginning to glimpse some home truths
about her work.

Women's work . . .

So what *is* women's work? It certainly isn't just paid employment.
Nearly all women do unpaid work as well, work that is necessary for
the survival of us all. In her book *Women's Work, Men's Work*,
Virginia Navarro describes the six tasks common to women in all
societies:

* bearing children
* providing food—preparing and serving meals and, in agricultural societies, cultivating food crops
* clothing people—by spinning, weaving and making garments

* tending to the frail and weak—small children, the elderly and disabled, the sick, and women in pregnancy and childbirth
* nurturing and educating young children
* . taking charge of the home—furnishing it, keeping it warm and clean.

Without these tasks the human race could not survive and the bulk of the work involved is done by women. As Virginia Navarro points out, the way this work is de-valued—the 'I'm just a housewife' syndrome—is a recent phenomenon. Traditionally, women have taken pride in the importance of their work. As Olive Schreiner wrote in *Women and Labour* in 1911,

> We knew that we upbore the world on our shoulders, and that through the labour of our hands it was sustained and strengthened—and we were contented.

In contrast, here a modern woman describes feeling a 'nobody' as a mother at home:

> No-one thinks you know anything if you are a housewife. They don't treat you as a thinking person, but as a right idiot. You don't need any qualifications for being a housewife, not like the doctor or the dentist or even a shopgirl, who's got experience, after all. You're just someone who looks after kids, and *anyone* can do that. Well, that's the idea, anyway.

Why do women at home often feel so unimportant? Well, the basic tasks have changed as some of the work has been taken out of the home. Industry now produces much of our food and clothing, and the state has taken over some of the caring and education. To some extent, this has freed women from the need for grinding survival work. On the other hand, it has robbed women of their traditional skills, and removed the control each woman exercised over her domain. Although she still carries the primary responsibility for the home, the work has been downgraded, isolated and trivialised. In addition, if she has a job outside the home she is likely to be doing work related to the same basic tasks. She may be serving dinners to other workers, making clothes in a factory or caring for the elderly in an old people's home. She is unlikely to be digging coal or managing a bank. In her job, too, she will find her work is poorly rewarded and of low status.

Over 60 per cent of women are employed in just ten occupational groups. In 1981, almost a quarter of all employed women were clerks, one tenth typists and secretaries, 7 per cent schoolteachers, almost 5 per cent saleswomen and shop assistants and just less than that nurses and midwives. Cooks and waitresses (3 per cent), cleaners and domestic helpers (3 per cent), packers, bottlers and canners (2 per cent) and welfare workers (2 per cent) come next. With the exception of office work, all are concerned with other people's need for education, food, cleanliness and care. (It seems reasonable to include shop work here because most of it involves distributing basic household items.) Office work, too, is servicing work—servicing administrators and managers. Overall, 75 per cent of working women are in service jobs.

Many of these jobs are in the public sector. The welfare state has transferred a lot of caring jobs from the home to paid employment— and the cutbacks are shunting many of them smartly back again.

The 25 per cent of women not doing service jobs are employed in manufacturing. Over half of them work in just four industries—food, drink and tobacco; electrical engineering; textiles; and clothing and footwear. With the exception of electrical engineering, we can again see a link with the basic 'female' tasks.

. . . and men's work

Men's work follows a very different pattern, and in spite of our equality legislation there is still a remarkable degree of separation between men's and women's jobs. 45 per cent of women work in jobs where there are no men at all. Only 31 per cent of women work in so-called integrated jobs, where not more than three-quarters of the workforce is of one sex.

Men are not concentrated in just a few types of work as women are; they work in a wide variety of industries and in the full range of white-collar jobs. Men also do far less service work, and a relatively small number of jobs related to the six basic tasks. They work on average much longer hours than women—few part-timers are male, and more than a third of manual men work over 44 hours per week.

Another important aspect of men's work, as Virginia Navarro notes, is their control of four significant areas—law and government; warfare; religion; and learning and the arts. Although these may exist in a primitive form in most societies, real development only takes place when some people can, through relying on the labour of others, remove themselves from the need to work on basic survival tasks. As slaves, wives or servants look after their needs, they have the spare time and resources for other occupations.

Most of these people are men, especially from the upper and middle classes. This certainly holds true in Britain today. All four areas are highly developed and women are conspicuous by their absence from all of them.

a) Law and government.   Margaret Thatcher not withstanding, most political power is firmly in male hands. 95 per cent of MPs are men. So are most senior civil servants, trade union leaders and industrialists. Not a single woman sits among the 288 male directors of the top 20 British companies. In the legal world, only 8 per cent of barristers and 3 per cent of judges are women. Very few industrial tribunals are chaired by women.

b) Warfare.   NATO, the armed services and the military-industrial complex are almost entirely male preserves. The women's armed services are small and play a largely servicing role. About 55 per cent of all research and development in the country is connected with defence—accounting for the employment of many thousands of (mainly male) scientists and technologists.

c) Religion.   Although more women than men practise religion, all the major faiths, including Christianity, are patriarchal organisations. Priesthood, and therefore entry to the hierarchies, has been forbidden to women. Despite continuing controversy, the men of the Church of England refuse to allow women to be ordained.

d) Learning and the arts.   Here, a distinction must be drawn between the education of young children—traditionally women's work—and the development of scholarship in colleges and universities. It is relatively recently that women have broken into this area at all. Women were not admitted to most universities until this century. A great deal of western learning and culture grew out of the monastic tradition, or relied on patronage from the rich; both established institutions that were predominantly male.

These traditions still underlie the pattern of jobs in education. Only 25 per cent of primary school teachers are men, but 57 per cent of secondary school teachers and 85 per cent of university lecturers are male.

It is these four areas, and not women's work, that society rewards with status, power and privilege. People who zealously pursue a career and reach the top (often brushing aside interests in home and family) are considered praise-worthy. They earn high salaries, knighthoods and peerages, and the chance of an international lifestyle—while women in essential caring jobs are rewarded with low pay and low status.

Taken for granted

The six tasks listed on page 45–6 are undoubtedly greatly under-valued in our society. As Dora Russell says: 'The prestige of masculine work has led women to despise and denigrate their own special contribution.' Studies of mothers at home with young children, for example, have found a depression rate of 30–40 per cent. The romantic image of motherhood is often a sick joke for mothers who feel they have no identity:

> To the people in the shop I'm just another housewife, to the people in the playgroup I'm just Tommy's Mum, to the people at Jack's work I'm just his wife, and I'm never seen as *myself*.

The work of feeding, clothing, and caring for people is taken for granted in most women's lives. It is 'natural', and so becomes invisible. Whether paid or unpaid, women are expected to get on with it, and receive little credit for, or support in, doing so.

Is there any sign of change? Is the separation of men's work from women's breaking down? Unfortunately not. According to a study sponsored by the Department of Employment, the pattern of women's jobs has changed surprisingly little since the turn of the century. In 1911, a fifth of female white-collar workers were administrators and managers. In 1971, the proportion was the same. There were more women in the higher ranks of the civil service in 1919 than there are today. Since 1911, women have made some inroads into the higher professions, notably medicine, but the proportion in lower professional jobs has decreased. In 1911, 24 per cent of skilled workers were women. By 1971, this figure had dropped to 13.5 per cent. Also, men have shown little sign of moving into women's jobs. The movement of men into nursing, for example, has been largely confined to the top administrative posts. And how many men can be seen at a sewing machine, cleaning floors, or teaching infants? Very, very few.

As for childcare and housework, there seems to be little hard evidence about men's participation. It is probable that modern husbands share household duties to a greater degree than before. But women still do the majority of the work and carry the overall responsibility. Women organise and men 'help'.

So women's continuing involvement in the six basic tasks is a crucial factor under-pinning the present pattern of work. It has two important consequences:

a) Where paid work has to fit in with unpaid work, a woman is restricted in her choice of jobs and hours of work. This in turn affects her wages, her promotion prospects and her time for trade-union activity.

b) The 'norm' of an eight-hour day and a continuous working lifetime applies to most men and few women. Many women spend a few years away from paid work while they have a family, and may return part-time for a number of years. As a result they lose out where pay scales are based on seniority and where promotion and training are dependent on long service.

We turn now to some specific aspects of the relation of women's work to women's lives: maternity and childbirth, caring for dependents, the experiences of part-time workers, and one of women's most persistent problems—low pay. In each case these two themes underly the discussion.

Mothers and babies first

When Judith, an ASTMS representative, asked her union college what accommodation they could offer her three-month-old baby while she attended a course, an official phoned back and said, 'I hear you've got a problem'. She was indignant—she had a baby, not a problem.

Pregnancy and childbirth is one part of women's biological inheritance that cannot be replaced or socialised away. Without it there would be no next generation. Yet it is often regarded as problematic because it disrupts adult activities and working patterns.

We have, of course, come a long way from the conditions pregnant women faced in the last century. Ivy Pinchbeck, in *Women Workers and the Industrial Revolution* quotes Betty Harris who, in 1842, described her work as a drawer of coal:

> I have a belt around my waist, and a chain passing between my legs, and I go on my hands and feet. The pit is very wet where I work, and the water comes over our clog-tops always . . . My clothes are wet through almost all day long . . . I am not as strong as I was, and cannot stand my work so well as I used to. I have drawn till I have had the skin off me; the belt and chain are worse when we are in the family way.

In 1915, the Women's Cooperative Guild published letters from working women about their experiences of maternity and childbirth. These letters, reprinted in *Maternity: Letters from Working Women*, revealed an appalling degree of suffering and exploitation:

> The first part of my life I spent in a screw factory from six in the morning till five at night; and after tea used to do my washing and cleaning. I only left two weeks and three weeks before my

first children were born. After that I took in lodgers and washing, and always worked up till an hour or so before the baby was born . . . I can only look back now on the terrible suffering I endured that tells a tale upon my health. I could never afford a nurse and so was a day or two after my confinements obliged to sit up and wash and dress the others.

These women would no doubt be amazed to hear that in the 1980s working women would have a right to six months maternity leave, a state maternity allowance and free medical care. Yet there are still many difficulties, especially for women trying to combine child rearing with paid work.

For much of this century, the ideal was the wife who didn't need to work because she was kept by her husband. In 1931, for example, only one in ten married women went out to work. Since the last war this has changed rapidly. Few women now stop work when they marry. Most stop at the birth of their first child and spend fewer years away from work than did their mothers. Five out of ten married women now work—a quarter of the total workforce. The tendency towards early marriage and small, planned families compresses child-bearing into a few years. Today, most women want a job for 30 or 35 years of their lives.

Mothers have a legal right in certain circumstances to return to their jobs up to six months after the birth of the baby. Some have no choice if they are to make ends meet. But most take a longer break. This may be for a number of reasons. A woman may not qualify for the right to return because she has not clocked up enough years at work. She may choose to spend longer at home, or she may fail to find suitable childcare.

As a result, there is a big difference between the employment rates of mothers and fathers. As *Hear This Brother—Women Workers and Trade Union Power* shows, 96 per cent of men and only 19 per cent of women aged between 25 and 34 work full-time. Another 24 per cent of women work part-time. In the 35–44 age group, the percentage of full-time women rises to 30 per cent, compared to 96 per cent for men.

Because women's working lives are interrupted, they fall behind in the competitive scramble for jobs. It is during these years that people in professional jobs expect to advance their careers. Salaries rise on incremental scales, so that every year the difference between the husband's earning power and that of his wife increases. He is also securing his pension rights and improving his chances of promotion.

In manual jobs, women's skills may become out of date. And if women want to go back part-time, they probably won't be able to use them anyway. They will have to take whatever job is available, however boring and badly paid. As Jackie, who lives on the outskirts of Glasgow, explains:

> I used to be a librarian, before the boys were born. Six months ago, I started on the twilight shift in the camera factory down the road. It's pretty routine work, inspecting lenses, but it's handy and I don't start till my husband comes in. He puts the boys to bed and I am home by midnight.

Legal maternity rights were introduced in the Employment Protection Act in 1975. This was a great step forward. But the rights are more limited than in many European countries and unsatisfactory in a number of ways.

Many mothers would like to take at least a year off, but if they do not go back to work within six months, they lose their job. In France, Austria and East Germany, mothers can take a year of unpaid leave. In Hungary, they can take three years. Some unions in this country have negotiated agreements for longer leave; a year in the publishers, Longman's, for example, and 90 weeks in the Open University. But the majority of British employers still only give the legal minimum.

Full-time workers only qualify for maternity rights after two years continuous service with one employer. Britain is the only EEC country to impose such a condition. Again, unions have managed to negotiate a shorter period with some employers. Women in the civil service, the Post Office and the Greater London Council qualify for maternity leave after one year. But many women are still prevented from taking up the right to return to their jobs because of the qualifying period. Part-timers working less than 16 hours a week are even worse off. They have to work for five years before they qualify. This kind of discrimination against part-time workers is very common. Yet it often goes unnoticed, and unions have done little to challenge it.

An employer is compelled by law to provide maternity pay for only six weeks. So, unless the union has negotiated a longer period of payment, women do not get paid for most of their maternity leave— hardly a desirable situation.

Finally, babies have fathers too. But there is no legal right to paternity leave. In Sweden, the 275 days leave may be taken by either parent, or shared between them. A number of unions here have negotiated one or two weeks paid leave for dads, though many major employers still give none at all. British Rail allows one day. Just long enough to learn how to change a nappy?

The lack of paternity leave is one example of how the odds are stacked against couples who decide to break away from the assumption that the women will stay at home. The tax and social security systems are others. These still assume women are financially dependent on men, so many couples lose money if they try to reverse roles. Also, the rigid distinction between full-time and part-time work makes it very difficult for men who want to share childcare to re-organise their working lives.

The 'norm' of continuous, full-time work is, in fact, a male norm. It discriminates against women by failing to accommodate one of the most important human activities—reproduction. This is not only a problem for mothers. Childless women often find that employers assume they are bound to want children sometime, or that they are less 'reliable' and less geographically mobile, simply because they are women.

Do we care about carers?

Although more married women go out to work than ever before, even more would if they could. A Gallup Poll published in *Women's Own* showed that 80 per cent of mothers want to work. A similar proportion said that they would want to work even if they were millionaires. So why do women stay at home? The answer, in a single word, is caring—caring for children, caring for dependent relatives and caring for husbands. Only a third of mothers with children under five go out to work, and most of these are part-timers. The bigger the family, the less likely the mother is to work. Also, as a survey in 1967 showed, one in five 'housewives' between the ages of 35 and 49 had a disabled person or someone over 65 in the household. And how many men still expect their wives to be, as the song says, 'a cook and a cleaner, a nurse and a maid'?

Carers may shoulder considerable financial, social and emotional burdens. They may have to sacrifice their own career and cope with a restricted lifestyle. For parents this may, of course, be the result of a conscious decision to start a family. But society certainly doesn't make it easy for them.

The rate of depression among mothers at home is alarming. Women do not want to work just for the money. They also need to stop 'climbing the walls' in the house. But the problem then becomes how to fit in work with family needs.

A survey of women factory workers, by S. Shimmin and colleagues, found that nearly all the women were in a semi-permanent state of stress. The constant anxiety and fatigue wasn't only due to their jobs, though these were boring and repetitive enough. It also arose from the difficulty of combining work with heavy responsibilities at home. This is women's 'double shift', described graphically by a machinist in a clothing factory near Glasgow:

> What do I do all day? Well, starting from eight o'clock in the morning, we work in here right up till five o'clock—well, we do when we've got work. Then I'm into shops, running in and out for my messages. Then by the time I've got them all fed and all washed there's all my housework to start. I'm lucky if I get sat down by ten o'clock, then a few hours sleep, and back down here again in the morning.

> It's all go, isn't it? You're actually doing two full-time jobs put into the one day. I mean, when a man finishes his work that's him, isn't it? He can put his feet up, can't he? But if you've got bairns you've just got to keep on and on!

And women doing the double shift are supposed to find time to be active trade unionists as well?

This essential caring work often goes unrecognised. Are feeding, nurturing and cleaning such natural activities that women who do them need no special recognition? Many women rightly dismiss this suggestion. They say, firmly and loudly, 'We're important', and they raise their demands—for proper childcare facilities, economic independence and a commitment to sharing from their menfolk.

Childcare

> Unions haven't done nearly enough to organise creches so women can have the freedom to work and not worry about the children. (Avril, AUEW)

> Why can't they have nurseries now? If there was a war tomorrow the women would be needed, so they'd get nurseries again overnight. (Angie, TGWU)

The war was the only period in recent history when nurseries were given priority, simply because women were needed to do men's jobs. Afterwards, as women were persuaded home to conform to the good housewife image of the fifties, nurseries were shut down. They have stayed closed. Today, there is a pressing need not only for nurseries but also for playschemes for the school holidays and facilities to bridge the after-school-to-five-o'clock gap. It has been estimated that these facilities exist for only 3 per cent of children. Places in private nurseries and with childminders far exceed local authority places. But the total is woefully inadequate.

The policy of the trade-union movement is to support local authority provision, though this support has had little concrete effect. Parents have also campaigned for workplace creches in several industries, notably education. At least 35 colleges have some sort of creche, though many are now threatened by the cuts.

The record of the trade unions themselves is poor. Until very recently, union events provided no childcare at all. Even now creches are limited to particular events in a few unions with vocal female memberships. Stories abound of childcare being badly advertised or poorly thought out. This is a sure sign that the issue is still not taken seriously. Facilities for members' children should be seen as essential. They should be as basic as travel arrangements, meals and toilets—and higher up the list than bars.

Financial independence

Financial worry due to the lack of an independent income is a familiar problem to carers. When a woman stops work to have a child, for instance, the family income suddenly drops just as expenses are rising. And it is no answer to say that families should rely on the man's wage to support them. This is no help to divorced women, widows or unmarried mothers. It is also no solution to families in which the husband is unemployed. The problem is not a new one. It was described by Eleanor Rathbone in the *Women's Year Book* for 1923–24.

> Indirectly [mothers] and their children in their infancy have to be provided for, and they have been provided for by the extraordinarily clumsy device of treating them as 'dependents' on men's earnings and roughly adjusting the latter so that it may be possible for wives and children to be maintained out of them. It is generally assumed that this is more economical than making direct provision, but as it involves the necessity of treating every man as though he were the head of the family and as though all families were the same size, it is really the cause of an immense waste and maladjustment of the world's resources.

To Eleanor Rathbone, the solution was to provide family allowances to mothers. She became a leading campaigner on the issue. In family allowances, she believed, lay the 'best hope that married women will at last achieve a position of real economic independence'.

Family allowances were first introduced in 1945, and have now been replaced by child benefit. But the payment has always been far too small. A sum that reflects the actual cost of bringing up a child is needed.

There is also the demand for a substantial increase in social security benefits, so that women who stay at home in a caring role are not financially penalised. Again, this means overturning the assumption that women are, or should be, financially dependent on men.

The trade unions have been slow to support these demands. Many negotiators cling to the notion of the family wage as a means of boosting men's earnings. The argument that this principle disadvantages everyone except male workers on good wages still falls on deaf ears. Yet this is a crucial issue for women, and one that deserves much wider debate within the trade-union movement.

Men's share

What about it, brothers, husbands, lovers? It is very simple. If you are not already doing it you will have to learn to clean the loo, cook meals and get stuck into the ironing. All without having to be asked. All without moaning, and without expecting to be thanked. OK?

> It is equality now you know—and I'm sick of telling him that. (Sue, NALGO)

> A lot of people think a wife should stay in and cook and have a meal ready for him when he comes home. I think that is ridiculous. I'd never do that. (Mary, AUEW)

Part-time workers, part-time rights?

Part-time work is the obvious choice for women struggling to combine family and domestic tasks with paid employment. Part-time work is not a problem in itself. In fact, it can be very liberating. Perhaps it is the ideal we should all aspire to, so that everyone, women and men, would have time to be with children, follow their own interests, *and* work. The problem is the way part-time work is treated in our society.

Women part-timers are regarded by employers as a reserve pool of labour that can be drawn on when necessary and packed off home again when demand falls. Part-time work is treated as second-class work with poor job security. It expanded considerably in the sixties and seventies as a way of tempting more married women into the growing service industries. It is now contracting again. Every cutback in the school meals service or in home helps costs women part-timers their jobs.

This is serious as part-timers need their wages as much as, if not more than, anyone else. After all, 86 per cent of part-timers are married women and 40 per cent of all working women now work part time. A woman does so because it is the only kind of work that will fit in with everything else. She does it because of other people's needs rather than her own.

Janet is a school cleaner in Glasgow. She works from six to nine in the morning and again from four to six in the evening. She has two children of school age.

> I'm out of the house before six. Then I come home in the tea break at seven thirty and wake them up for school. The work is just round the corner so there's no travelling. That's why I could take it.

She leaves breakfast on the table with a flask of tea, so that the children don't have to use the stove, and goes back to work. At lunchtime, she is home to feed the children, do the washing and prepare the evening meal. At four o'clock, she goes back to work. After school, the older girl copes until Janet comes home and gives them tea. 'I'm exhausted when I get home. It's such a full day.' She is well aware of the limitations of the job, and of why she does it.

> If you need the money to keep the house going, you have to go to work, and you go out with worries in your head about what's happening to them. I don't mind the work, but I'd like a more interesting job. A cleaning job is just like being at home. It's no change, you're just doing it on a bigger scale. I'd like to do something or achieve something constructive.

How typical is this experience? When a woman looks for a part-time job what can she expect?

Her pay will be low.   Women's earnings are lower than men's, and part-timers are lower still. In 1980, according to the Department of Employment's *New Earnings Survey*, the average hourly earnings of non-manual women working full-time was £2.21 compared with £1.83 for part-timers; and the average hourly earnings of manual women working full-time £1.72 compared with £1.54 for part-timers.

Low pay rates are partly a result of the fact that part-timers lack bargaining power as relatively few are in unions. Most unions have also been slow to take up part-timers' problems. Many part-timers also lack information about minimum rates set by wages councils (if there is no union how are they supposed to find out?). Others fear losing their jobs—especially now, when new jobs are so hard to find.

Her choice of jobs will be limited. Women's work in general is concentrated in a few areas, and part-time work is even more so. The *New Earnings Survey* found 37 per cent of part-timers in cleaning, catering, hairdressing and other personal services, 20 per cent in clerical work, 14 per cent in professional work like nursing, and 11 per cent in shop work. In other words, the pattern is overwhelmingly of service work in women-only jobs. In these ghettos of female labour, women have little chance of training or promotion, and few opportunities for taking responsibility.

She will have fewer rights. In employment law, everyone working over 16 hours a week has the same rights, thanks to pressure from the TUC. (The previous cut-off point was 21 hours.) People working between 8 and 16 hours do not. They have to clock up five years' continuous service to qualify for rights given to other workers after one or two years. Maternity rights, periods of notice, unfair dismissal and redundancy payments are all affected. This discrimination against part-time workers serves to reinforce the myth that this work isn't really important.

Part-timers often miss out on access to pensions, and on holiday and sick-pay arrangements too. Also, 'part-timers first' has been a familiar cry during redundancies. But a successful tribunal case has now challenged this practice. Sandra Powell and Brenda Clarke, part-time workers in a Birmingham factory, claimed their redundancy agreement discriminated against women. The tribunal agreed with them, and the case sets a useful precedent.

So the low status of part-time work is yet another aspect of the low status given to women's work, both paid and unpaid. Unions could do a lot more by taking up part-timers' problems and recognising they have as much right to their jobs as everyone else. But the only long-term solution is to break down the distinction between part and full-time work. The shorter working week is a step in the right direction provided it is not made up with overtime. So is the fact that job-sharing is at last being taken seriously by some unions and employers. These are important developments. They help to stop us seeing part-time work as marginal. They also, in theory, make it possible for men to take a real share in childcare and so begin to lift the burden of the double shift from women.

End low pay!

Women's work still lags behind men's in pay as well as in status. The relative position did improve in the early seventies when the Equal Pay Act was coming into force. But a gap still remains. There are two reasons for this. Firstly, a woman can only claim equal pay if there is a man in the same job. This leaves thousands in women-only work unaffected. Secondly, equal pay could not compensate for the concentration of women in the lower grades of both manual and white-collar work.

Since 1978, the gap has been opening up again, as the graph below shows.

Women's hourly earnings as a proportion of men's, 1970–79

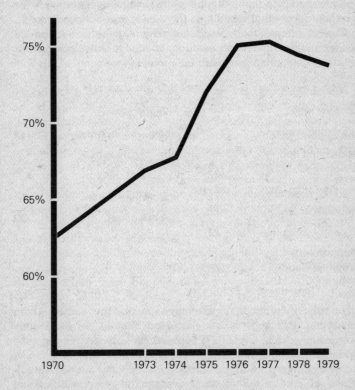

Source: derived from the Department of Employment's *New Earnings Survey*, 1970–79.

If we compare average *weekly* earnings, instead of hourly rates, men are even better off in relation to women. This is because of extra payments for shifts and overtime. In April 1981, according to the *New Earnings Survey*, the average weekly earnings of women in manual jobs was only 62 per cent of men's earnings in manual jobs (£75 compared with £121) and of women in non-manual jobs only 59 per cent of men's earnings in non-manual jobs (£97 compared with £163). If we look at selected occupations we see, for instance, that women primary teachers earn 87 per cent, women shop assistants 65 per cent and women in catering and cleaning 69 per cent of what men in the same occupations earn.

So women's pay is still very poor relative to men's. The table below gives a comparison that is starker still. It compares the rewards for high-status jobs with the earnings of women in essential service work. The figures are from the *New Earnings Survey*, which unfortunately does not publish the salaries of the even more lucrative positions of barrister, judge, cabinet minister and company director.

Average gross weekly earnings, selected occupations

Full-time men		*Full-time women*	
University academics	£297	Nurses and midwives	£94
Finance and tax specialists	£245	Nursing assistants	£80
		Cooks and chefs	£72
Personnel managers	£218	Sewing machinists	£66
Police inspectors	£222	Kitchen hands	£62
Company secretaries	£214	Waitresses	£62
Scientists and mathematicians	£188		

Source: Department of Employment, *New Earnings Survey*, 1981.

The majority of workers classified as low paid are women. There are several definitions of low pay. Here we will use the Family Income Supplement level of £75 per week for 1980, and for part-time workers the pro-rata rate of £1.90 per hour. The percentages of men and women over 18 years old earning less than this are very revealing. In the case of full-time male workers, 16 per cent of manual workers and 10 per cent of non-manual workers (1.4 million in all) are low paid. For full-time women workers the low paid figures soar to 70 per cent of manual workers and 49 per cent of non-manual workers (or 2.6 million in all). Furthermore, 68 per cent of all part-time women workers (or another 2.5 million) are low paid. In all, 5.1 million women—out of a total female workforce of 8.4 million—are low paid by the government's own criterion.

Traditional wage bargaining is quite unable to tackle this problem. The aim of maintaining differentials only helps higher-paid workers—mostly men—and locks women in low pay. Comparability studies do little better. How does it help a hospital cleaner if her wage increase is based on the pay of her sister cleaner in a hotel? Comparing like with like means comparing women's jobs with women's jobs, and low pay with low pay. And as for the type of payments bargained for, flat-rate increases are rare, yet percentage increases serve only to maintain the gaps.

We will not reduce the inequality between men and women's pay until women's work is given greater value. To do this, we will have to break away from trapping women's work in female ghettos. Job segregation between the sexes goes hand-in-hand with low pay for women—a chicken and egg situation the Sex Discrimination Act has proved totally unable to deal with.

This brings us back once again to the problem of trade-union representation. While negotiating priorities are determined by higher-paid workers and are strongly influenced by sectional interests, we are unlikely to see the fundamental shift in bargaining aims which women want. Low pay is one of the clearest indicators of women's lack of power in union negotiations and policy-making.

Old problems, new pressures

So far, this chapter has looked at the long-standing features of women's work. Now, the problems of the eighties are bringing new pressures to bear in a number of ways. The post-war expansion of women's jobs has stopped. Recession has taken over. Unemployment is growing, and new technology is changing many of the jobs that remain. State facilities for the old and the young are being reduced. All these developments affect women, both at home and out at work.

'I want to work'

As unemployment has rocketed in the last few years, women have fared very badly. Women's unemployment has been growing at a faster rate than men's. Between January 1976 and January 1980, male unemployment actually declined by 2 per cent from 942,000 to 926,300. Female unemployment rose from 254,000 to 412,000—an increase of 62 per cent. The proportion of women among the registered unemployed continues to increase. There are also hundreds of thousands of women available for jobs who do not register as unemployed while they are at home. In 1981, the total number of working women fell for the first time since the fifties.

Women have been caught by the economic and technical changes causing the present tragedy of unemployment. Jobs in manufacturing have been dwindling for years, but in the fifties and sixties the loss was offset by an increase in the number of jobs elsewhere. Local government, the health service, education and service industries like banking were all growing. A textile worker who lost her job could re-train as a typist; a machinist could find work as a hospital auxiliary.

Now, the decline in jobs in factories has accelerated and the alternatives are running out. Public expenditure cuts have hit employment in every service controlled by national and local government. Staffing levels in hospitals are being reduced. Nursery education is under attack. The school meals service is being drastically cut. Residential homes for the elderly are being closed. These cutbacks mean more unpaid work for women. They also mean fewer paid jobs, particularly for part-timers. Between June 1979 and September 1980, part-time work in local authorities was cut by 7 per cent, compared with a 1½ per cent cut in full-time jobs.

On top of this is the job loss due to new technology. Gone are the days when every mother could advise her daughter to learn shorthand and typing so that she would never be short of a job. Clerical unemployment started to increase rapidly in the mid-seventies as the earlier boom in office work slowed down and stopped. At present, 90 per cent of women working in offices do routine clerical and typing jobs. It is these routine jobs which are most under threat from computer systems. When records are computerised, one woman can do the job of several filing clerks. With a word processor, one operator can do the work of three or four typists. Any work that involves dealing with information—whether in the form of accounts, records, customer details or words—is at risk. The job of a computer is to manipulate information, and to do it faster, more accurately and more cheaply than a human being.

In 1978, a German company, Siemens, shocked the white-collar world with a forecast that 40 per cent of all office jobs in Germany would be carried out by computers by 1990. Some recent forecasts for Britain are not much more comforting. The clerical union APEX predicts a loss of a quarter of a million typing and clerical jobs by 1983. Clive Jenkins and Barry Sherman of ASTMS calculate that 30 per cent of all information processing jobs will be lost by 1990.

New technology is also changing the nature of many office jobs. Although computers create a few highly skilled jobs, it is more common for automation to de-skill workers. The machine takes over the more complex and interesting parts of the work, turning them into standard routines. Advertisements for word processors, for example, claim that an inexperienced typist is able to produce the same quality of work on the machines as a skilled secretary. She no longer needs the skills of page layout or judging paragraph lengths as the machine does it all automatically.

The familiar problems of the production line—a lack of control by the worker and pacing by the machine—are creeping into many women's white-collar jobs. And the economics of automation demand that machines are used non-stop. A CIS report, *The New Technology*, described the working conditions for the operators of word processors introduced in Bradford council:

> The machines are in constant operation and are programmed by the rate material comes in. The workers have one ten minute break in the morning and afternoon, and otherwise have no contact with other workers during office time. All new work comes in through a special anti-static glass box, and no non-section workers enter the room.

In other words, the once easy-going office has been transformed into an assembly line for words.

New technology does not only affect office work. The distributive trades are being changed by computerised stock-taking and automatic checkouts. Many factory jobs are also at risk. In particular, repetitive assembly, packaging and inspection tasks are prime candidates for automation. Betty, for example, works in a factory making paper products and is well aware of what is happening:

> I work at the end of the line, wrapping and packing the toilet rolls. It's boring, soul-destroying work. Every time there is a new bit of machinery, two or three more women lose their jobs. They're gradually squeezing the women out of here. They say they must have people with mechanical experience to work on the machines, but we haven't got that.

'But unemployment isn't a real problem for women, is it? There's always the housework to do.' Such damaging myths are not uncommon, in spite of having little truth. Women need their wages. And many women, like men, suffer boredom, depression and a loss of self-confidence when they become unemployed. As Jean, a word processor operator, says:

> I want to work. I don't want to go on the dole. It's like someone telling you you're no good any more. You're not wanted so off you go, toddle off somewhere.

Where is there to go? The problem can be particularly acute for young people who have never worked and wonder if they ever will.

> I spend the day doing me Mam's housework. Oh, I don't mind doing it. It's something to do. If I didn't have something to do I think I would kill meself, I'd be that bored. (Deb, aged 19)

> It's just horrible not having anything to do. People call us, saying we are scroungers and that, but I'd rather be working, and so would everyone else, I think. I've been down to the Job Centre loads of times but there's never anything in. There's just nothing. (Jeanette, aged 18)

Jobs for the girls?

Although some people still churn out the old view that married women should give up their jobs for other people, it is unlikely that many of the unemployed would be prepared to do the jobs most married women do. It is hard to visualise redundant steel workers or young men out of school doing cleaning or nursery nursing. (They wouldn't accept the low pay anyway.) The greatest threat to these jobs is recession in industry and cuts in public services. Some women's jobs may, however, be in danger from male competition in a recession. These are the mixed jobs—administration, teaching, computer programming and semi-skilled factory work. Ideas of equal opportunity are easily branded as a luxury when people are fighting for their jobs. When costs are tight it is harder to argue for special facilities like nurseries that would make it easier for women to work.

So unemployment and the effects of new technology are undoubtedly making the pursuit of equality at work more difficult. APEX's comment about the effect of office technology might well be applied more widely:

> The freedom which employment opportunities give to women is fundamental to the achievement of full equality. Thus any tendency for office technology to turn back the clock on women's employment would be a profoundly disturbing social development.

Is the trade union movement up to the challenge? Present day problems are an exacting test of the strength and political will of the trade unions. A central part of the test is whether they are prepared to defend women's interests and women's jobs—and this will depend largely on the extent of women's power and strength in unions.

Women's work, women's lives

This chapter has been about women's work and women's lives and how the two are wrapped up together. Most women cannot conform to the ideal of an uninterrupted working lifetime or to the ideal of continuous trade union membership. Instead, mothers and carers have to maintain a precarious balancing act between the demands of their dependents and the need to earn a wage. The 'Needs and Opportunities' grid (below) summarises the distribution of basic survival tasks among adults of working age, and shows how this influences both their choice of job and availability for trade-union activity.

Needs and opportunities

	People affected	*Job choice*	*Union activity*
Group 1 People who look after the needs of others	Mothers, women with dependent relatives, a few fathers.	At home, or part-time job, or highly stressed with full-time job.	Very little time. Almost impossible in evenings, at weekends or overnight.
Group 2 People who see to their own needs.	Women without dependents, childless couples who share housework, some single men.	Can usually manage a full-time job.	Can find some time. Weekends and overnight may be difficult.
Group 3 People who have someone to see to their needs.	Most married men, rich people who can pay others, some young people living at home.	Full-time job.	Can manage heavy involvement, including nights and weekends away from home.

This grid highlights an important reason for the absence of women from the higher levels of unions. Being a full-time official or a national executive member involves nights and weekends away from home and many evenings out. In other words, it demands a lifestyle only easily achievable by those in Group 3—the lucky ones who can arrive home after a meeting to find the kids tucked up in bed, a meal ready and a clean shirt for tomorrow. Even people in Group 2 may find this lifestyle difficult. Who is going to get the shopping in and feed the cat while they are away? It may not be enough to be free of dependents; you really need someone to look after your daily needs for you. The only women who are in this position are the very few who can afford to pay someone to look after the house or the children.

Many trade union posts are too demanding for most people to cope with. This is especially true for women. Perhaps executive and official posts should be job-shared and more effort made to negotiate time off for meetings in working hours?

The grid should also make it clearer how women's struggles grow out of women's lives. To women in Group 1 it is more important to defend childcare and welfare services than to boost differentials and overtime rates. Many women in Group 2 rely on birth control and abortion facilities, and on equal pay at work, to maintain a degree of choice about how they live their lives. It goes without saying that there are hardly any women in Group 3, yet our society relies on this group for most of its decision-making in industry, government and the trade union movement. These high status positions are only realistic for people who do not have to spend a lot of time looking after their own, or other people's, basic needs.

It seems crazy to regard this as the norm. Yet that is the hidden assumption behind the pattern of men's work; the idea is that men do the real work while women service them. Our real challenge must be to turn this assumption on its head. We need to stress the value of the basic survival tasks, and we need state support and men's participation to share them out more equitably. We also need flexible working time to make this possible. Finally we need a trade-union movement that realises the importance of these issues and is prepared to fight for them.

5.
Equality–
Fighting for the Dream

When women workers see things about their lives that are unjust or wrong, how do they fight for change? The simple answer is: in every way possible, from industrial action in factories to national negotiations and lobbies of parliament. But a more complete answer can be found in the long and difficult struggle for equal pay. This was a significant campaign for women, a symbol of the whole fight for equality.

Equal pay is a powerful and emotional cause for women. To be doing the same job as a man and to be paid less than him simply because you are woman is humiliating. It is to be told you are not worth much, you are not important. Why else would you be paid less in a society which equates money with value? Unequal pay for equal work is a blatant sign of women's oppression. As such it has been an important target for women to organise against. Women workers might well borrow the advice given by Lillian (see page 42 above) to a Youth Opportunities worker:

> I says, don't *ever* feel ashamed. If you're doing a good job of work and you are getting a quarter of what you are entitled to, don't feel ashamed. Feel angry, but don't feel ashamed.

Women were angry, and fought for equal pay in every way they could. Three main areas of activity emerged. These were: negotiating with employers; applying political pressure; and campaigning for equality legislation.

It is useful to look briefly at traditional union attitudes to these three areas. British unions have always relied heavily on direct negotiation with employers as the best means of improving their members' pay and conditions. They generally regard the law with suspicion, or see it as irrelevant (with the exception of special areas like health and safety). Most unions condemn government attempts to control pay through incomes policies as 'interference', and regard free collective bargaining as the ideal.

This freedom to negotiate, to join in the hurly-burly of the annual wages round, is fine for workers like miners or dockers who know they can cause a lot of economic damage with a strike. It is also fine for people at the top of the pecking order for wages—the skilled men in a factory, and the higher grades in a profession. These groups have bargaining power. Women often do not.

Bargaining power is an important concept. When a union team faces management across the negotiating table, their chances of pulling off a successful deal depend on two things:

a) Their economic power.   The union is in a relatively strong position in any of the following circumstances: when the employer's business is healthy, so he can afford to 'buy off' union demands; when the union represents workers in an economically vital industry such as steel, electricity supply or coal; when there are shortages of labour or of particular skills; and at times when the employer does not want to risk a strike.

b) Their trade union power.   The more united the membership, and the stronger their feelings about the issue, the more pressure the union can apply to the management. As a TGWU delegate explained at the TUC's equal pay conference in 1973:

> If we stand up and demand, then we get somewhere. You know this as well as I do in regard to employers. You know that you go in and negotiate and they look over your shoulder—and the extent to which the lasses and lads are behind you is the extent to which you can get a concession in your wage negotiation.

Women workers may lack both economic power and trade-union power. Clerks and cleaners cannot bring industry to its knees in a few weeks like steelworkers and railwaymen can. Semi-skilled part-timers are more easily replaced than skilled men. Nurses and primary school teachers have less political clout than medical consultants or university professors. And when it comes to trade-union power, particularly over equality, can men be relied on to unite with women and support their demands? Are the (mostly male) union leaderships commited to bringing women fully into the union organisation?

Sadly, the answer is 'not necessarily'. Men and women in mixed workforces are not always united. And as for priorities, a study by researchers at the London School of Economics for the Department of Employment (Research Paper 20), into the implementation of the Equal Pay and Sex Discrimination Acts found that for most union negotiators equal pay was 'a minor issue, peripheral to their central concerns and worries'. Problems to do with inflation, recession and the fear of redundancies were judged to be more pressing.

Yet unions have continued to tell women that bargaining is best. A typical comment was made by the General and Municipal Workers Union to the Equal Pay and Opportunity campaign in 1977:

> We have always taken the view that the best means to achieve equal pay is through collective bargaining and that the law shall only be used as a last resort when all else has failed.

This is all very well, but how many women would still be waiting for equal pay if we hadn't had an Equal Pay Act? And to take another example, if we didn't have legal maternity rights, how many unions would have given priority to negotiating a maternity agreement instead?

Women have learned the hard way that bargaining is not enough. They had to bring both political pressure and the law into the fight for equal pay. Neither of these removed the need for bargaining, but they gave women more bargaining power. Political campaigning helped to swing public opinion in women's favour. And the law made equal pay a necessary bargaining aim and backed it up with a threat of legal sanctions.

Let's now look at how this worked out in practice.

An early victory

The first significant equal pay victory was won through a political campaign in the fifties. This was for equal pay for civil servants and teachers. Men in the civil service generally supported the women's claim, but the National Association of Schoolmasters vehemently opposed equal pay in teaching. It would be unfair to the dependents of married men, they argued, for single women to be paid the same as men. (There is, however, no record of a similar attitude to single men.)

The campaign was launched with a big parliamentary lobby in 1951, organised by women MPs. The activists leading the campaign chose political pressure as the most appropriate method of achieving equal pay. There was little experience of industrial action in this largely white-collar workforce. Moreover, the government itself was the civil servants' employer, against whom the campaign was directed.

The cause quickly gathered strength in the relevent unions and among sympathetic MPs. The TUC gave its support in 1951, in spite of some reluctance from the General Council, which retained a ƌference for collective bargaining. In 1952, the decision to campaign politically was vindicated when the Burnham Committee, which negotiates teachers' wages, decided not to concede equal pay until the government did so.

By 1954, the campaign had intensified. Local committees organised protest meetings; demonstrations and lobbies of parliament continued. Two petitions were handed in to the government. One received considerable publicity as it was delivered in three horse-drawn carriages decorated with the colours of the suffragettes.

Shortly afterwards, the Chancellor of the Exchequer announced that equal pay would be implemented in teaching and the civil service over a six year period. It was a victory for women. Political campaigning had achieved in four years what half-hearted negotiations had failed to achieve in as many decades.

It was, however, essentially a white-collar victory. It had been helped by arguments about professional status and the growing demand for teachers and office workers. Most manual women still did not have equal pay. Progress through the TUC-preferred channels of collective bargaining was painfully slow. A questionnaire, sent to 49 unions by the TUC General Council in 1962, revealed that only 19 had equal pay agreements. Half of these were in the civil service, and none of the unions without agreements was optimistic about future prospects.

Slow progress

Although the TUC had adopted the principle of equal pay in 1888, there had always been a tension between two different views of equal pay amongst male trade unionists.

On the one hand, trade unions rely on collective strength and solidarity. Men's ability to protect their own wages is undermined if employers get away with paying women at a lower rate. Men may therefore support equal pay as being in their own interests. A good example of this comes from the first world war. In Newcastle upon Tyne in 1915, women were asked to volunteer to work on the trams. The only snag was that the employer offered them 15 shillings a week, when the men's rate was 28 shillings. The men refused to let the women take the jobs unless they were paid the full rate. The employer eventually agreed to do this, so the women got their 28 shillings and, we are told, they all joined the union.

On the other hand, some men respond to the idea of equal pay by keeping women out, or by making sure they are kept in separate jobs so that they do not undercut the male rates. Here is the experience of

Gladys Rushman, a village postwoman, interviewed in 1970 by Mary Chamberlain for her book *Fenwomen*:

> I'm what they call an auxiliary postwoman. When they take you on, being a woman, they don't take you on as a full employed person . . . So we get paid less than a man—very definitely. I was really a bit annoyed about that when I knew.
>
> I'm not a member of a union, for the simple reason we're not expected to join, auxiliary postwomen that is. Of course, all the official postmen do, they're all in a union. But they don't ask the women to. Funny, but there . . . I suppose it's because, really, you're only an auxiliary. It's a sort of vicious circle really. Since we are not allowed to join the union, we can't push in to make suggestions.

Some men have found it hard to shake off traditional ideas about women's role. There was, for example, little chance of equal pay for female railway clerks when, as late as 1946, their union voted to retain the marriage bar. Sarah Boston, in her history of women in trade unions, quotes the argument that won the day:

> If true family life was to be restored in this country and a halt called to the falling birth rate and the growing number of unhappy marriages women must leave the service on marriage and devote themselves to the important task of home-making.

Women have been used as scapegoats too. 'Division, segregation, amalgamation, redundancy, and most of our present ills are traceable to the policy of employing less men and more women', raged the general secretary of the Post Office Workers Union in 1935—an attitude hardly likely to increase women's confidence in the union's commitment to equal pay.

In industry in the early sixties, women's demands for equal pay often went unheeded as it was a period of rapid wage advance for men. Full employment and a shortage of skills, particularly in engineering, resulted in an upsurge of workplace bargaining as groups of workers negotiated payments far greater than the nationally agreed rates. This was the era of 'you've never had it so good', when the media portrayed an image of a new labour aristocracy cashing in on the consumer boom, filling their houses with stereos and driving fast cars.

Of course these highly paid workers were mostly skilled men. Most manual women were still earning less than the average unskilled male. Their frustration erupted at the TUC in 1963, when a motion from USDAW called, for the first time, for legislation on equal pay.

Two years earlier, the USDAW conference itself had glimpsed women's impatience. A grocery store manageress had torn up the union's report on equal pay during her speech, exasperated by the lack of a wholehearted campaign for equal pay in shop work.

At the TUC, USDAW's motion was passed and it became TUC policy to campaign for an equal pay law. It was a significant turning point. By calling for legislation the unions were overturning their previous faith in collective bargaining. They were acknowledging that bargaining had failed to secure equal pay, and that a law was needed to back up the campaign.

Congress also adopted a six-point Charter of trade-union aims for women workers. This was:

* Equal pay
* Opportunities for promotion for women and girls
* Improved opportunities for training young women for skilled work
* Apprenticeship schemes for girls in appropriate industries
* Re-training facilities for older women who return to work
* Special care for the health and welfare of women workers

It was no accident that three of the six points referred to training. Equal pay would be meaningless unless it was backed up with equal opportunities. Education and training were vital if women were to overcome their disadvantage at work.

'Determined not to give in'

But years of battle still lay ahead. The Labour government of 1964–70 included a commitment to equal pay in its manifesto, but did little to help during its early years in office. The TUC continued to be soggy on the issue. In 1966, it reported that 'Equal pay, despite the proposed tri-partite meetings of unions, employers and government representatives, still seems a distant prospect'. Women delegates at the annual congress were not amused to discover that the General Council had sent an all-male delegation to the preliminary discussions.

Two years later, women at Ford's Dagenham plant struck the spark that ignited a new surge of militancy among women, and which resulted in parliament passing the Equal Pay Act in 1970. Two hundred women brought the massive car factory to a standstill when they walked out over management's refusal to consider their re-grading claim. They were skilled machinists and they wanted parity with the men. The AUEW made the strike official, and after three weeks management conceded a sevenpence an hour rise, taking the women to 92 per cent of the men's rate.

It was a strike that captured women's imagination. As Barbara Castle, whose intervention helped to settle the dispute, commented in a speech:

> Let us salute these lasses. They were determined not to give in, though they were desperately hard up and their family lives were almost broken up.

The Ford strike was one of the events that heralded the re-emergence of the women's movement in Britain. And it marked a change of approach by the people leading the struggle for equal pay. Sarah Boston explains:

> The approach of 'relying on male colleagues', waiting 'for social attitudes to change', or leaving it to collective bargaining to grind its way towards equal pay over several more decades was rejected. Legislation would have to force equal pay to be negotiated; it would have to lead, not reflect, a change in social attitudes.

In 1970, the Equal Pay Act was at last passed, though it was not to come into force until 1975. During the intervening years there were six attempts to introduce an anti-discrimination law as well. In 1973, the Labour government agreed in principle to such a law, and the Sex Discrimination Act was passed in 1975.

The laws at work

It was the end of one long period of struggle and the start of another. Equality did not, and could not, happen overnight. The principle of equal pay for similar work is simple enough in theory, but putting it into practice is riddled with difficulties and pitfalls. Trade-union women were well aware of this. In a debate at the TUC women's conference in 1972, a teacher had warned delegates of the difficulties:

> If you believe that once the Equal Pay Act comes into force you can afford to rest on your laurels because the fight is won, let the women teachers, from their own experience, disabuse you of that misconception. We have experience of equal pay over a decade and with increasing bitterness over those years we have come to realise that the establishment of a principle by no means guarantees its fair and equitable application, and anomalies still exist in our salary structure.

Enforcing a law against discrimination presents even greater problems. Discrimination is hard to pin-point and difficult to prove.

Why then were the two acts important to women? For two main reasons:

a) The acts helped to raise women's expectations about their work. They could now argue that equal pay and opportunities were theirs as of right. And attempts to implement equal pay taught women a lot about employer and trade-union attitudes towards equality. This period coincided with the sudden growth of ideas about women's liberation, ideas which filtered into unions and caused many women to look around them with new eyes.

b) Workers could use the acts as powerful negotiating tools to deal with grading structures and payment systems which left women in second place. The combination of strenuous negotiations and legal rights is potentially a strong one—when a union chooses to use it.

But many problems arose in the wake of the acts. Many lessons emerged about the usefulness (or otherwise) of the law and of collective bargaining. Let's now turn to the post-1975 period and draw out some of its main features.

Where were you, brother?

Passing a law on equal pay did not remove the need for bargaining. If anything, it was now more necessary than ever. Employers had five years to implement equal pay, so they had plenty of time to work out how to get round it. A vigilant union was the only protection against their avoidance tactics. True, women's pay did rise significantly during this period (see page 59). But a woman's right to equal pay depends on her job being the same or broadly similar to that of a man, or being rated as equal in a job evaluation scheme. The law did not touch women-only jobs, and for women in mixed jobs the loopholes turned out to be enormous. Small differences between jobs could be created to make sure they were not 'broadly similar'; employers could grade heavy work higher than detailed work to justify men's differential; or they could simply stop recruiting women in certain areas.

Union negotiators often let them get away with it. The Department of Employment study (Research Paper 20) of equal pay in 26 organisations reported that 14 employers had taken action to reduce their legal obligations. In every case, lack of pressure from union representatives was a crucial factor.

> In some cases, union representatives and many of their members were hostile to equal pay. It was seen as a threat to men's pay and jobs . . . The worst examples of [minimising] action appear to have been taken not only with union knowledge but in certain

cases with union collusion and pressure . . . Pressure was put on management in some organisations to ensure that existing differentials were restored where men's and women's rates had been equalised.

The kind of management action taken with union consent in three of these companies is shown below:

Action to reduce equal pay obligations

Type of agreement	Action taken
1. Industry agreement for manual workers.	Tightening of women's payment-by-results rates during implementation. Male labourers put on bonus scheme to raise earnings levels.
2. Collective agreement for manual workers.	Parent company created grades specially so that women would not be equalised. Higher grades were for heavy work, lower ones for light work.
3. Job evaluation agreement for manual workers.	Men moved off night work and other areas of work to prevent equal pay comparisons. Introduction of job evaluation scheme: all female jobs (bar one) in lower grade; that is a *de facto* women's grade. Piece work rates, previously sex-linked, now for heavy press work and light press work.

(Source: Snell et al, *Equal Pay and Opportunities*, Department of Employment Research Paper 20)

This study showed how easily employers and unions can brush aside women's right to equal pay. And it demonstrated that male workers' claims to support equality for women are meaningless unless they are prepared to give up some of their relative advantage. It is not possible to have both things at once.

Relying on ourselves

This rather dismal picture is cheered by accounts of the workplaces where women took up the fight themselves, sometimes with the support of their union, and won some notable successes. In some factories where women were well represented, good equal pay agreements were made. Harriet, for instance, (see page 85) regards negotiating equal pay for her women members as one of her greatest achievements as a convener.

When bargaining broke down, industrial action followed. One of the most famous disputes took place during the summer of 1976, in the Trico factory on the outskirts of London. Four hundred women in the US-owned windscreen wiper factory won equal pay after a five month strike. Support flooded in from women's groups and trade union branches as well as from their own union, the AUEW. The women's claim had been dismissed by an industrial tribunal half way through the strike but, undeterred, they stayed out and won.

My Song Is My Own includes this *Song for the Trico Women Workers*:

> The management are not prepared
>   To give us what we ask.
> They are saying that they can't believe
>   We're equal to the task.
> But if men can do what we do
>   Then their argument's a farce
> So we want equal pay.
>
> The tribunal's decision
>   Came out the other day,
> And we were not at all surprised
>   By what they had to say.
> They didn't give us what we want
>   So out and out we stay,
> Till we get equal pay.

Sometimes men supported women's action; at other times they did not. At Salford Electric Instruments in Lancashire, women workers went on strike in 1974, after management refused to give them bonuses equal to the men's. The men carried on working. 'We are absolutely disgusted with them', said a shop steward. 'We are feeling bitter about it.' After ten weeks, the women returned to work with higher bonuses and a new sense of unity and strength, but feeling suspicious of the men—a good example of how a split between men and women weakens a union for the future.

In contrast to this, men employed by Cockburn's Valves in Paisley joined the typists and comptometer operators when they struck for equal pay in 1976. The lowest-paid male clerk, who could not type, was being paid £50.83—£10 more than the typists and £20 more than the lowest paid clerkess. 'We couldn't have survived without the support of the men', said one of the women on the picket line. (*SR* 47)

Equal pay would never have been achieved without women activists. Because of women's relatively weak position in union hierarchies, a lot of hard campaigning at the top was carried out by a small number of women. There was also an important grass-roots role for the activists. Some groups of woman workers feared equal pay. They were frightened of losing their jobs if they had to compete on equal terms with men. The apparent security of their separate, lower-paid work was tempting. Women who had moved beyond this fear into political understanding and action played a vital role in persuading their sisters to do the same. As Mrs Sabin of the GMWU said at the TUC equal pay conference in 1973:

> There are a lot of people like me. I think I am entitled to equal pay, that it is my prerogative and my right, but there are still women who say 'I will lose my job and I would rather work for £2 less and keep my job' . . . Now I have tried to the best of my very humble ability to get it into these people's heads that this is their right, that they will not lose their jobs, because any shop steward worth her salt will not allow it to happen.

The need for women's activism and persistence was far from superseded by the advent of the equality laws.

A suitable case . . .

How much help is the apparatus of the law itself? Women can take complaints about equal pay and discrimination at work to an industrial tribunal, and unions can refer discriminatory pay agreements to the Central Arbitration Committee for amendment.

One or two tribunal cases have gone to appeal and have set important precedents. (Tribunal decisions themselves do not constitute legal precedents, only appeal cases do.) Belinda Price brought a case against the civil service on the grounds that the age bar of 28 for executive officer posts discriminated against women because so many mothers were taking a break from employment over those years. Her case was successful and the civil service had to phase out the age requirement. Recently, the case brought by two women in Birmingham (see page 58 above) found that it is illegal to make part-timers redundant first.

But overall, the tribunals have played a very minor role. The number of cases has been small. Only a minority have been won. (Relatively few pay agreements have been referred to the Central Arbitration Committee either.) And under British law, cases can only be taken by individuals. We have seen none of the spectacular class action suits brought in the United States against major companies on behalf of all their female employees. In one famous case, women and ethnic minorities employed by the giant American Telephone and Telegraph Company won an agreement giving them a total of £50 million in back pay for past discrimination.

There are a number of problems with the British tribunal system, in particular the small number of cases. 1976 saw the largest number of equal pay cases, 1,742 in all. The total has fallen annually, and was down to 91 by 1980. Each year, over half the cases have been settled by conciliation (with what results for the women, we do not know). A number of others are always withdrawn. Of those that reach a tribunal, the success rate has never been higher that 30 per cent,and by 1980 it has fallen to 15 per cent—a total of just four successful cases!

The number of hearings about sex discrimination at work has been even smaller, even though this covers such important areas as recruitment, promotion and training. In 1976, the first year of operation of the Sex Discrimination Act, there were only 243 applications to tribunals. In 1980, there were even fewer—just 180. (By way of comparison, the number of unfair dismissal cases each year is about 35,000.) Here too the success rate is low. Of the 69 cases which went as far as a tribunal hearing in 1980, only 14 were won.

The small number of cases does not mean that discrimination or inequality no longer exists. It simply shows how difficult it is for women to translate their experiences into cases that will stand up under the law. And as there is no legal aid for industrial tribunals, women who are not union members may have to go to a tribunal without any legal advice and conduct their own case—another factor that is bound to put women off.

Why then do women lose cases? Trade unionists tend to mistrust the law when it relies on the interpretation of words like 'reasonable', 'suitable' and 'broadly similar'—words which can mean very different things to a worker, an employer and a lawyer.

If a woman thinks her work is broadly similar to a man's, will the tribunal agree with her? The interpretation of this phrase has varied enormously. Unions and watchdog organisations like the National Council for Civil Liberties have criticised tribunals for dismissing cases on the grounds that minute differences between jobs meant they were not broadly similar. The following case is an example:

> *Bowden versus CWS Ltd.* Ms Bowden was a telephone saleswoman for a fruit and vegetable depot. She claimed equal pay with two male telephone salesmen. They all telephoned custom-

ers, taking orders and trying to increase sales. The work was exactly the same except that the men sometimes spent a few minutes each day working out premiums and discounts on the phone for customers. Also, if a customer called in person they would be received by one of the men. The tribunal ruled that the men's work was more demanding than Ms Bowen's and her case was dismissed.

Cases are also lost if the employer can prove there is a 'material difference' which accounts for the pay differential between the man and the woman. This is to allow for factors like seniority and skill level which might result in two *men* being paid differently. But this phrase too has been interpreted in variety of ways, as these examples show:

Parsons versus Gomshall and Associated Tanneries. Mrs Parsons was employed as a sales clerk. She dealt with UK sales and claimed equal pay with a man in export sales. The firm agreed the work was the same but said the man was paid more for merit reasons. The tribunal disagreed and awarded Mrs Parsons equal pay.

Hobson versus Rowntree Mackintosh Ltd. Mrs Hobson operated a machine which wrapped boxes of Black Magic chocolates. She claimed equal pay with men working on machines which wrapped Kit Kats. The tribunal ruled that because the men were handling unwrapped chocolate bars and the women were handling boxes of chocolates, the men's 'responsibility to their employers with regard to the product, which goes to the customer, is therefore of a different nature from that of the applicant'. The case was dismissed.

Needless to say, this sort of result is not likely to encourage other women to bring cases.

If it is difficult to win a case for equal pay, it is harder still to prove discrimination. Pay differentials are at least visible. Discrimination often is not. It may be a matter of attitudes, and it is difficult to collect hard evidence for a case.

The problem was recognised by the women's advisory committee of the TUC in its attitude to proposed anti-discrimination legislation in 1972. In its report to that year's women's conference, the committee recognised that a law might eventually be necessary, but 'their general view was that they would prefer to remove discrimination without legislation—primarily because they were not convinced that it could be effectively enforced'. An employer might have to advertise for 'salesman/women', but how could a union hope to control the conduct of the employer during the interviews? Girls wanting to become mechanics now had to be considered for courses, but educational traditions meant few girls would apply for this sort of course anyway.

It was clear that the new law against discrimination would not make everything instantly rosy for women. It could not remove people's expectations about the 'proper' roles of the sexes. A thousand and one forms of sexism carried on happily, untouched and unchallenged by the law. Even the courts and tribunals seemed to be bound by stereotypes. In the first discrimination case to go to the Court of Appeal, Lord Denning announced that the 1975 Act did not 'obliterate the differences between men and women or do away with the chivalry and courtesy which we expect mankind to give womankind'. He apparently did not appreciate how often people try to justify discrimination with excuses about chivalry and the need to protect the 'weaker sex'.

The case taken by women customers in El Vino's wine bar in London was a classic example. Although this was not an employment case, it is interesting as an example of an unhelpful legal attitude. Four attempts have failed to stop El Vino's policy of serving women only if they are seated and not if they are standing at the bar. Judge Rankin dismissed the case in the County Court, saying that the practice had existed for many years and only a handful of people would find it objectionable. The court failed to understand that this example of chivalry *was* discrimination because it meant treating women differently from men, and in a manner they objected to.

A sacked TOPS student had the same trouble persuading an industrial tribunal to accept her experience as discrimination. Helen Sanders enrolled on a carpentry course. She was dismissed after a three week trial period on the grounds that she was slow and her work not up to standard. Helen felt that 'Women who have got through the courses have been brilliant—I'm average. Women should be able to be average. If a man had produced that quality of work he'd not have been thrown off the course.' (*SR* 99) The instructor had given her a strength test, which the men didn't have. She felt isolated and undermined on the course. She also said women were indirectly discriminated against because they were less likely to have previous experience of woodwork. The tribunal disagreed and dismissed her case.

Finally, the law does not prevent discrimination against lesbians. In 1981, Susan Shell was sacked from her job as a care attendant in a girls' hostel because of her sexuality. There had been no complaints about her behaviour or her work—Barking Social Services just didn't like the fact she was a lesbian. NUPE backed her case of unfair dismissal to an industrial tribunal. She lost, as the tribunal held that she would 'offer a bad example for the girls to model themselves on'.

A long way to go

The British equality laws have failed to break down traditional views of appropriate work for men and women. They have given only limited help to women trying to overcome their low status in the labour force. Job segregation and low pay are still the norm. Many problem areas remain to provide a challenge to women and their unions in the eighties. Some of the main ones are as follows:

* Blatant discrimination still occurs, though it may be hidden. The LSE team in their study for the Department of Employment (Research Paper 20) found managers in 22 out of 26 organisations who admitted that they had discriminated or would discriminate over promotion, hiring or training of women. In several cases, they were under pressure from shop stewards to keep women out of male areas or prevent women supervising men. But people have learnt to cover up. No interviewer is silly enough today to say, 'Sorry, you won't get the job because you are a married woman'. Instead, they will say, 'Sorry, you don't have enough experience' or 'Sorry, the competition is very intense'.

Managers are mostly very ignorant about the equality laws, according to the LSE study. Many thought the laws were irrelevant because 'we already have equal opportunity here'—in spite of clear evidence to the contrary.

* Indirect discrimination is still a big problem. The conditions attached to some jobs make it difficult for women to do them. Married women, for instance, cannot easily move around the country or attend residential training courses. Traditional promotion paths are often a barrier. Supervisors in industry are usually promoted from the skilled sections. Chances are few in the unskilled and clerical areas where women predominate. In professional and academic jobs, women may be excluded from men-only clubs and dinners and they may not have time to join in the drinking and rounds of golf that are important for 'getting on'.

* Myths about women's inability to do lifting and heavy work are still common. Memories appear to be too short to recall the jobs women did during the war years. One-third of companies questioned by the LSE team blocked women from higher-paid jobs because managers believed they couldn't physically cope with the work. In fact, very little heavy work was usually involved. The real problem was that managers assumed women are all the same, instead of giving each individual the chance to see whether the job was suitable for her.

* Women are protected by law from doing night work in factories (though exemptions can be granted). This keeps women out of some jobs, but the question of what to do about it is controversial. The Equal Opportunities Commission favours repealing the protective laws; the TUC is in favour of retaining them and aiming, eventually, to extend them to men.

* Special provision for married women is still almost non-existent. Removing overt discrimination is not enough. There is a crying need for re-training for women returning to work after bringing up a family. And for many more jobs to be available on a part-time basis. One hopeful sign is that one or two unions have taken up the idea of negotiating 'family responsibilities leave', to enable parents to take time off to look after sick children without losing wages or risking their jobs.

* Inequalities in education and training are still enormous, and underlie the distinction between men's and women's work. Hairdressing is the only apprenticeship done by girls in any numbers; girls take less day-release than boys; the woman on a technical course is still an exception. Employers and educational bodies have made very little use of the provisions in the Sex Discrimination Act which allow for positive discrimination in training to boost the numbers of women in traditionally male jobs.

* The government neatly exempted itself from a large part of the anti-discrimination legislation by leaving out tax, social security and pensions. So women's supposed equality at work is maintained against a background of gross inequality in these essential financial areas, making it difficult to get rid of the assumption that women should be financially dependent on men.

In spite of some real gains, women are still plagued by inequality. What then has been learned in the years of struggling for equality at work?

The fight for equal pay taught new generations of women the lesson their mothers and grandmothers learnt through campaigns for the vote and birth control, for entry to the professions and the abolition of the marriage bar—that an advance for women is rarely given gladly. Women have to fight for it. The battle is usually hard and long, and sometimes bitter. As the socialist Stella Brown said in 1922: 'It was never safe for groups of women to trust to the gratitude and justice of groups of men. Women must organise in their own interests.'

For women in the trade-union movement, the years of campaigning clearly showed their lack of trade-union power. Most unions consistently failed to give equal pay sufficient priority in negotiations. In workplaces, male union leaders often failed to prevent divisions between the workers along sex lines which weakened union claims for equality. The scarcity of female officials made it difficult for women to do anything about these problems.

Collective bargaining, the bread and butter of union activity, turned out to be at best an unreliable, and at worst a useless method of achieving equality for women. So women had to fall back on legislation which would force both management and unions to adopt equal pay as a bargaining aim. To get the legislation women fought a vigorous campaign to convince people of the justice of their cause and win support in parliament.

But here was the paradox. As trade unionists know, the law by itself is not a magic potion for change. It is no more than words on a page until it is enforced. And who was to enforce equality at work? It was up to groups of women and their unions again. There are no equality inspectors to patrol employers like factory inspectors do for health and safety. The police will not march in and prosecute an employer for an act of discrimination. The only effective enforcement agency is the workforce. An employer who keeps women down will continue to do so just as long as the employees and their union let him. With the law behind them the workers are stronger, but it is still their action that counts.

Women's action did result in real gains. Women's pay rose relative to men's in the early seventies. Attitudes and expectations changed. The idea of equality for women became much more widely accepted. Many blatant examples of discrimination were eradicated.

The campaigns also brought out some lessons for the future. They showed how important it is to have active women in the TUC and at a national level in unions, women who can campaign politically when progress at the grass-roots is slow. The fight for equal pay showed that trade-union power matters. And that powerlessness will continue to be problem for women in unions, until there are more women in membership and a greater number in key positions in negotiating teams and union leaderships.

Women's trade union power will never be fully realised until male and female workers cease to be divided by mutual suspicion and differing priorities. Such divisions do not only disadvantage women. They weaken every mixed workforce and therefore the whole trade-union movement. The strains of economic crisis can easily sharpen divisions, so there is at present an urgent need to work towards unity.

So how are we going to improve the lot of working women in the eighties? The new rallying cry is 'Positive action now!' Positive action in trade unions is needed to boost women's involvement and emphasise women's interests. Positive action at work could delve into the roots of inequality and take action to pull them out. The last chapter assesses the achievements of positive action and the tasks that remain.

6.

Portraits

Harriet Vyse: 'Looking after my women members'

Harriet Vyse (née Hopper) has been an active member of the AUEW for 24 years. She was the first woman to be elected onto the union's National Committee. How did it all start? 'Well, it sounds trivial, but it was all to do with the toilets!'

In 1957, Harriet was working in a Cosmos factory in Sunderland, testing radio valves. None of the women in her section was in a union. They were not allowed to smoke on the job so it was common practice to go to the toilets for a cigarette. The foreman complained about the number of women going at one time, and brought in a rule that the workers had to ask whenever they wanted to go to the toilet.

'There was one woman in our section, she was in her fifties and a terrific personality, a proud woman. One day she made herself ill rather than having to sink to asking. Well, that was it. We just blew up. Three of us went and told the foreman we weren't going to put up with it.'

They won and the matter was dropped. A few days later someone from another department came round with application forms for the engineering union. They all joined immediately, determined never to allow the same sort of thing to happen again.

Harriet was asked if she would be prepared to be the shop steward. 'I don't know if it was conceit or lack of understanding, but I said yes and that was the start of it.' She was 26, and felt very green about union matters.

'The first case I had was about the merit system. Two girls had been missed off the award, so I went up to the desk with them to see the foreman. All I got out was, "Mr Parry, these two girls haven't got their merit award." He just looked at me and said, "It's got nothing to do with you, you go away and I'll deal with these two." I turned round and walked away and thought "I'm not making much of a job of this". Then I met our late district secretary who said, "Look Harriet, carry on, because if you fall flat on your face I'll be there to pick you up". So I decided to stick with it.'

The union grew in strength and within a short time all the women were in membership. But soon her section was threatened with closure. She found a job in a nearby factory, which was shortly afterwards taken over by Plessey.

After a year there Harriet's shop steward resigned, and she was the only one prepared to take over. What made her take on the demanding role of shop steward again?

'I don't know really. I've never felt afraid to meet people and talk to them, and I think I've always been the sort of person that has wanted to see justice done. I think I got a sense of satisfaction out of being needed.

'I have to go back to explain. When I was about nine I weighed less than three stone because of my spine disease, caused by a fall downstairs when I was two years old. When I went to school I was very tiny and weak, and I would have fallen down over a matchstick. I can remember thinking I was going to be a burden, and as quick as the thought came into my mind there was the determination that I wouldn't be. I think it was that instinct that kept me going. Also I became much stronger health-wise with the loving care from the family.'

Once Plessey took over, the union had to become better organised. They were now part of a multinational company in which the old-style management had been replaced with a new structure. Out of twenty-one shop stewards seven were female, representing women in semi-skilled and assembly jobs. The women became dissatisfied with the convener and wanted to nominate Harriet in his place. She resisted for two years as by this time she was branch secretary and felt that enough of her time was spent on union matters. But after some of the other women stewards threatened to resign if she didn't stand, she relented. Much to her surprise, the shop stewards elected her as their convener by a majority of two votes, making her the senior trade unionist for the 900 AUEW members in the plant.

'The reaction from the women was great, but the reaction from the craftsmen! They wouldn't even accept a semi-skilled convener, but a woman! Well, it was just not on, and I was told in no uncertain terms straight after the meeting by the tool room steward that they wouldn't accept me.'

The next few weeks were unpleasant for Harriet as she tried to establish herself in the role of convener. Her worst time was during the annual wage negotiations, when the craftsmen insisted on putting in a separate claim—something that they had not done before. Harriet arranged a mass meeting for the craftsmen to discuss proposals to put to the management, and the men threatened a walk-out.

'I never slept the night before the meeting, and I thought, "Well, if I back down now I'm going to let all the women down, and no way can I do that, so I'll just have to ride it". I remember I got a cup of coffee out of the machine, and by the time I'd got to the meeting hall, which was about ten yards away, there wasn't a drop of coffee left in the cup—my hands were shaking that much. I was literally terrified. Anyway, I didn't let them see it. I dropped the cup before I went in.

'So I went inside and all the stewards were there. I got as far as saying, "Right, we've called you together this morning . . . " Then one of the fitters said "We're not stopping", and they all walked out. A few more followed them, and I thought, "Youse can walk out, but I'm not". Then there was a voice from the back saying "Never mind, Harriet, we're still here", and honestly, I could have run up and kissed that fellow!'

After that, relationships began to improve. At her union women's conference, Harriet asked another woman convener how she managed. She replied, 'It's damned hard. You've got to prove yourself, but once you have proved you can do the job, it's OK.' Harriet agreed. 'I'd certainly say I earned the respect of the majority of the craftsmen, but I had to make sure I did my job really well.'

She was convener for two years, until the tool room steward stood against her and was elected. The achievement in which she takes most pride was negotiating an equal pay agreement for the women in June 1975. There were other big issues too, one of which blew up into a strike. Management planned to introduce a system of patrolling supervisors. The workers were strongly opposed to the idea and went on strike after negotiations broke down. They were out for seven days—until the management agreed to have ordinary supervisors instead.

'I certainly wasn't strike-happy, but there comes a time when you've got nothing else left. Some people think you can solve everything by talking, and you know it just doesn't work out that way. Employers will keep you talking till the cows come home. They'll give you all the cups of tea you want so long as production is going on downstairs.

'Some people say women are not militant—well, they are. They will sit calm and put up with a hell of a lot, but once they are stirred up . . . We had some laughs too, though. I remember when 42 women in the machine shop were fighting for equal bonus and about 60 of us came out in support of them. I'd stopped up all night and made all these posters. I'd started one in big letters saying NO SEX DISCRIMINATION, but I couldn't get discrimination in in big letters so I wrote it smaller. One of the women, who was a real rough character, says "I'm not carrying that, they'll kill us". "What for?" I asked. "Look at the way it reads—NO SEX." I never realised!'

Meanwhile, Harriet had been elected onto the AUEW's Joint Divisional Council for the north-east, on which she was the only woman. Then in 1973 she became the first woman to be elected onto the union's National Committee as a full delegate. She received a standing ovation at the annual conference when the result was announced, though some union members were less enthusiastic. 'Some comments were that it was a gimmick of the north-east. But I don't accept that. I mean, I got there on my own qualifications and experience, and I know I didn't let the women down. But what upset me more was that no other women followed me from the other regions. I thought there might be two or three women the next year, but it's just never happened since, which I think is a pity.'

So did she want to go any further herself? 'I was never ambitious to become a full-time official or anything like that. I had no desire to move up the ladder, and it's not because I was afraid I wouldn't be elected. I was content just being on the shop floor. To me the most exciting part of being in a union is on the shop floor. My first instinct was to look after my women members, and the more knowledge I could gain, the better I could do my job.

'Then again, I lived at home with me Mam, you know, and no way did I want to leave home. Fortunately she had good health and I had sisters nearby, so I could go away to conferences and that. But I just loved being with her. So as for district secretary, I wouldn't have thought about it.'   As someone who gained considerable personal support from the AUEW women's conference, Harriet supports some special measures for women in the union. 'Oh yes, I agree we need positive action for women, and women's courses. I still think we need women's conferences until we know that attitudes have changed and we are going to get a fair hearing at national level. I'm not sure how I feel about creating positions at executive level. But we need a voice at the top, and if this is the only way we are going to get it, then we've got to grab at everything.'

She's sure that if women on the shop floor saw they had more leadership at a national level it would give them more confidence. If more women were involved 'you would see a big change in working conditions, especially in the health and safety area'.

Does she think she has been influenced by the women's movement? 'Looking historically I think I was very influenced by the suffragettes. I can only sing their praises because of what they went through to get us the vote. The women's movement is fighting all sorts of causes, and they are necessary. But to be perfectly honest I am not sure what a feminist is, what it means.'

She has always believed in the importance of men and women working together. She wouldn't have achieved what she did without men's support. The employer is the opposition, not other trade unionists. 'It grieves me sometimes when there is this split. We had the split when women were getting less money, and we've got it still between craftsmen and semi-skilled. But when you've got men and women against each other it is just a ploy, you know, for the employers to use. Simply, I feel that as workers we need each other and should try and be tolerant with each other's faults and insecurities.'

Now Plessey in Sunderland has closed down. After a period on a MSC-sponsored health and safety project, Harriet faces the prospect of unemployment again. How does she feel now, looking back?

'It was hard work, there's no argument about it. I've travelled to London and back overnight to attend meetings and I've sat up till four in the morning doing branch work. I don't know where I got the energy from, though I got a lot of support from me Mam. But I'd do it all again. I don't regret anything. It was all worthwhile, and I met some fantastic people.

'The satisfaction you get from being able to do something for your members—I dunno, it is something money just can't buy.'

Barbara Gunnell: 'Questioning the whole notion of leadership'

Interviewed by Eva Kaluzynska

Barbara Gunnell is 35, working as a freelance journalist specialising in development issues. When she joined the National Union of Journalists 12 years ago, it was in an unorganised workplace producing reports on industrial relations, and she became active almost immediately, helping to form a chapel. 'This was at the time of the Industrial Relations Act, which my work involved monitoring. My politics started to evolve from that, given trade union resistance to the Act, and from my own membership of the NUJ. Before that, I'd been doing some work on the effects of equal pay legislation and on the employers' attempts to juggle pay scales to avoid its intentions, for a magazine.'

Soon Barbara and others from her chapel became involved at branch level. Magazine Branch currently has just over 4000 members, organised in 72 chapels. About half its working members are women. The branch has had a good record of participation by women, right up to national level. Both the first woman president (the only one so far) and the current chair of the union's powerful Standing Orders Committee, which organises the business of the annual conference, came from Magazine Branch.

Barbara was elected to the branch committee, and started to build experience of the union nationally through attending annual delegate meetings. 'Magazine Branch was unusual in that there were so many women involved. The branch committee had a majority of women on it when I joined it, and for much of the seventies, I think. Individually, most of those women would have described themselves as feminists, and were fighting feminist battles elsewhere, but within the branch itself, we were probably a bit complacent.

'Looking back, it's clear that men dominated all the debates, and probably chose the subject matter, deciding what was "important" and being willing to declaim about it. I've heard since that women who are now very active in the union were put off for years by the heavy "macho" style of politics during that era.'

Magazine Branch was renowned as a left-wing stronghold at the time. The International Socialists were a dominant influence, and IS's successor, the Socialist Workers' Party, still has a strong presence in the branch. 'The sexual politics of the International Socialists—I was a member at the time—have always been a little suspect, and way behind those of the International Marxist Group, for instance. On the other hand, the IS line always emphasised genuine rank and file involvement, working in chapels. At that important level, most magazine activists seemed to be women.'

This was the background for the left of the branch arguing against NUJ involvement in the TUC women's conference. The NUJ had traditionally tended to vote against ghettos for women's issues. 'I had reported the TUC women's conference a couple of times and found it a most dispiriting event. Every vote was unanimous. The leadership seemed utterly sycophantic to the men at the top and quite incapable of changing anything. So I wasn't very sympathetic to the idea that the TUC women's conference should be used as a forum for feminist debate, particularly as the push for it seemed to be coming from a very middle-class element in the NUJ with no background in work-place trade union activity. In fact, they were freelances, so they didn't have workplaces.'

By the time Barbara decided to stand for one of Magazine's two seats on the National Executive in 1978, she had done most chapel and branch level jobs, and had been elected to two important nation-al working parties, the first to investigate the union's finances, the second on new technology.

'When Rosaline Kelly, who had been the union's first woman president, decided to leave the executive after many years of service, I felt very strongly that the branch should send another woman to join it, rather than leave both seats to men. I'd had plenty of the right sort of background, and I couldn't think of any reason why I shouldn't stand.

'The first person I told was a close woman friend and a seasoned NUJ activist, and I remember thinking she reacted as if standing for the NEC was something women didn't do.' This was, of course, historically true. Barbara spent her two years on the executive as the only woman on it.

'Perhaps it isn't so much the case now, but I felt that there were people who behaved at branch as "future NEC members". They were all men, making the right speeches and behaving in a generally patrician fashion. All you had to do was ask them to stand. I found it worrying that both men and women seemed uneasy about a woman—me—standing. It was almost as if I were doing something impolite!'

But the climate of opinion was changing. Some women activists saw themselves as both feminists and trade unionists, without ranking those strands of activity, though there were divisions, with some feminists unwilling to identify with the left, which they distrusted deeply. 'Women who thought of themselves only as feminists and not as socialists treated me as if I were a surrogate male on the executive, and I resented that strongly.'

Barbara was disappointed that they failed to recognise the poten-tial of a woman ally on the NEC who would have been able to support them more effectively on issues they wanted raised if, for instance, the Equality Working Party of the time had consulted or briefed her. It didn't. 'Looking back, I think that was rather sad. Whatever their assumptions about my views, I think they should have tried to establish a cooperative relationship. More recently, the Equality Working Party has very consciously developed a role in supporting women already in office, as well as working to get better women's representation.'

What was a two-year stint on the executive like as the only woman among 22 men? 'The biggest problem was fitting into that very male type of behaviour expected of executive members on a large, formal committee.' Meetings are long, and there is the ceremony of members standing to speak, making points of order, displaying debating society techniques. Women who had never been privy to such an occasion were astonished to hear from Barbara of the issues our executive sometimes deemed worthy of such dignified treatment.

There was, for instance, the time the NEC spent almost an entire half day of its precious two-day meeting debating, in all seriousness, the possibility of removing ceiling tiles from its meeting room. And a past president told Barbara with amazement that he once changed his mind on an issue after she put her point of view. This, she feels, reveals far less about her powers of persuasion than it does about the rigid postures her colleagues generally adopted in debating.

'It's all performance. There's no doubt that dramatic skill is valued very highly by most male trade unionists—think of the televised bits of the TUC. Most women feel that speaking isn't something they're particularly good at. I spoke very little at meetings. I'd only intervene if I had a new, specific point to make, but I think that was probably interpreted as me not having much to say and being rather feeble. Everyone else seemed obliged to intervene on every debate, even if someone else had already said the same thing. So we'd have tremendously long set-piece debates with each member standing up in turn to make their speech. And sometimes the president would congratulate us all on what a fine debate we'd had, while I'd simply be annoyed at the self-indulgence and the amount of time we'd taken over a decision.'

How do we change that? Barbara doesn't have an answer, but is convinced that while such behaviour is part of the job description, few women will be tempted to apply. What with the workload, threat to career prospects—especially if one is inclined to the left—and disruption to private life, relatively few members compete for the privilege anyway. For women, with added difficulties over securing a tolerable career, during which many have to juggle that and children, the prospect seems doubly remote, 'so only the really "odd" ones try'.

Barbara was perturbed by the degree to which one has to be 'odd' to consider standing for the executive. She is not married and has no children, both factors deemed odd for a woman. She considers the executive workload as 'ludicrously high' and felt that a two-year stretch was about as long as most people could manage to do the job properly 'without degenerating into a hack'. Being on the executive certainly didn't enhance her career prospects. The year after her term of office, she decided to opt out of constant friction with a none too benevolent employer, and became a freelance.

For 1981–82, there are two women on the executive, both in their second year of office. Neither had to contest her seat. One is from Magazine Branch, and Barbara made a point of encouraging her to stand. Two other women contested seats and lost. A conservative electorate voted for conservative candidates in a secret ballot. So although the NUJ's membership is 30 per cent female, only two out of 23 NEC members are, and there have never been more than two women on the executive at once. Barbara is unsure about the best way of challenging that.

'I've read of the way women in other unions have used special seats and benefited from them and I'm persuaded completely that they've been the right thing for those unions. I'm not sure about pressing for them in the NUJ. If those women had lost because they were women rather than because of their politics, I'd have said we should consider special seats. But I think they're daft as a doctrine if you don't go further and question the real reasons women won't stand for election, like the ludicrous hours that you can't combine with job and family, and the male atmosphere. One or two women with special seats wouldn't change that. It's the NEC system that needs changing. I found it appalling that a long-stand male NEC member supported special seats rather than encouraging one of the many good women activists in his branch to take over his seat.'   As for women's committees, Barbara still feels there are dangers in segregating issues specifically to do with women members, both as workers and as trade unionists. Such committees can allow an executive to feel absolved of any responsibility for women members, and they frequently lack the authority to implement changes. But she considers the work of the Equality Working Party to have been useful, particularly of late, as it has tried to address major debates on the future of the union from the point of view of its women members.

Barbara sees the development of an informal sector as one of the most valuable sides of feminism emerging as a potent force in the union. Networks of activists—and friends—have been built up throughout the country and in the different sectors the union covers. They have linked women and sympathetic men over issues affecting women, and helped ensure a women's presence in a broad range of union affairs. 'For example, discussions we've had in the London women's group radically changed my views on several issues. My thinking on special seats and on the need to change the NEC springs from those meetings. And women in the NUJ have been way in advance of men on issues and problems arising from proposals to amalgamate with the National Graphical Association.'

But Barbara is unhappy at the lack of support, even informally, for women who reach high office. 'I'm not sure why this happens. Women trade unionists are good at encouraging women to take office at the bottom of the union and at helping new office holders. But some of us seem distinctly uneasy, nervous, about seeing women at the top. I have felt that it almost amounts to hostility, and I think my successor on the NEC has been feeling that too. I don't know why there should be such unwillingness to support someone who's done something we apparently want women to do.'

She concedes that part of the problem may be that mutual support tends to depend on shared experiences, and at the moment few of us know what the pressures of being on a union executive are like. 'It could also be that men get that disapproval and hostility all the time but don't mind, while women can't be that thick-skinned. After all, they aren't used to being in the firing line.'

Barbara feels that men in the union have changed considerably over the period in which she has been active. Some feminist ideas have gradually become seen as commonsense, and feminist women have been involved in union struggles of all kinds, resisting being labelled a fringe interest group, so men 'just can't pretend those ideas don't exist' any more. Nevertheless, she suspects that with many men, the apparent change of heart has more to do with expediency than with genuine conviction.

She would like to think her term on the NEC had helped to make women in the NUJ think 'that standing for the executive wasn't something outrageous for them to do', and hopes they won't be deterred by the prospect of losing elections.

'I think the major contribution of feminist thought in the NUJ has been to make us question the whole structure of meetings, executives, the whole notion of what leadership is. I really think that if three or four of the women who have been involved in this process were to get on the NEC, it would have a dramatic effect on the way that body behaved. The meetings might become less pompous, more efficient, shorter, and more women might feel more inclined to try it.'

7.

'We're out to right the wrong'—Through positive action

In 1972, the TUC women's conference debated a proposal to wind itself up. The motion began with these words: 'Conference considers that the continuance of a separate women's conference is inconsistent with the trade union ideal and policy of equality for women.' It was neither the first nor the last of similar debates, but it took place in an interesting year. The Equal Pay Act had been passed by parliament and would come into force in 1975. Women knew they had won something of a victory. So was the idea of a separate conference an old-fashioned hang-over, out of place in the new era of equality dawning for women? Or was it as necessary as ever to have a place where women could come together and gather their strength for the continuing fight for equality?

The latter view prevailed, the motion was lost and the women's conference survived. But it is interesting to consider the arguments used in the debate. Trade unionists are still discussing the issues and applying them to the whole range of positive action measures used to overcome the barriers to women's full participation in unions.

The main argument against the women's conference was that it increased the division between men and women, which was something people were trying to get away from. 'We are not *women* trade unionists. We are trade unionists and I ask you to support this motion.' The speaker felt that keeping women separate from men only confirmed their second-class status.

'We have got to deprive ourselves of this annual outing to pleasant seaside towns', argued another. 'We shall miss a trip, but what shall we get in return? We shall start treating ourselves as equals: never mind waiting till they start treating us as equals.'

While they acknowledged there were far too few women at the full congress of the TUC, the opposers of the women's conference believed that women simply had to get stuck in and prove they were as good as the men. Women accepted their role as victims too easily. As a NALGO delegate put it:

> Women are conned from the cradle to the grave that men are their superiors and it is up to women to take the wool from their own eyes . . . If we cannot take our rightful place in the TUC with the men behind us, it is our own fault so let us take our fingers out and get on with it.

Two women argued that the conference didn't have much effect anyway. It had too few powers; it could only pass resolutions on to the women's advisory committee or to the general council of the TUC, which often ignored them.

> We do not have the right at the moment to act on our own decisions and, therefore, if you think you are giving up anything much at all, just get it very clear that you are only giving up an advisory service. That is all you are getting under this women's conference.

The majority of the speakers—who clearly reflected the dominant mood of the conference—disagreed with all these points. The women's conference was still valuable because equality had not arrived. Women's problems were not going to vanish with a law about equal pay. An AUEW-TASS delegate effectively summed up the argument:

> We believe that while the fight for equality continues it is most important to continue holding these conferences . . . Equality has not yet been achieved and it is not likely to be achieved completely for some time. Until the time comes when women have gained their rightful place in society, we think it is important for women to have a separate women's TUC conference where problems particularly appertaining to women can be discussed.

How did the conference help? Well, it acted as a meeting place for active women. Here, they could listen to other women's points of view, talk over problems and get 'inspiration to carry on the fight'. For many women, the conference was a stepping-stone to further union activity. This is an important argument for positive action—it is much easier for women to learn to value themselves and to increase their knowledge and experience through women's activities rather than in mixed groups. A delegate from SOGAT explained:

> It is mainly through the women's conference that we can keep the active women interested, educate them and so get more

women onto the committees on the shop-floor, at the branches,
onto district committees, executive councils and, finally, onto
the male-dominated TUC.

A shop workers' delegate backed up this point, arguing that a lot of
activists would not have become leaders without the women's conference to help them. 'Women can come to this conference and get
confidence for themselves by speaking to their own kind.' Compared
to this, speaking at full congress as one of 50 women among over a
thousand men was 'quite an ordeal'. There, said a delegate from the
Bakers Union:

> Marvellous speeches are made by general secretaries or the
> district secretaries of unions and after hearing them you feel you
> cannot find anything to say, but here tolerance is the key word.

Finally, some delegates disagreed with the view that the women's
conference was powerless. After all, women had very little voice
anywhere else in the TUC. Out of the 50 women at the previous
year's congress, only five had spoken in the week-long proceedings.
The women's conference might not be listened to as much as the
participants would like, but it did allow women to form policy on
important issues. A delegate from Leeds Trades Council put her
view:

> The value of this conference lies in the reflection within the
> trade-union movement as a whole of the decisions, the advice
> and the excellent contributions we get here.

Since the 1972 debate, the women's conference has flourished.
And there has been a sudden growth of other forms of positive action
for women in unions. By the late seventies, it was clear no new era
had dawned as far as women's pay and choice of jobs was concerned.
Women had also made little progress towards getting a fairer representation in their unions. But one thing *was* changing. A new generation of feminists from the women's movement was becoming active in
trade unions and some were finding a voice at the TUC women's
conference. They were mostly in white-collar jobs—teaching, journalism, local government and the civil service—and they brought a
fresh approach to the old arguments. They brought a strong message
from women's liberation to trade-union women: we need women's
groups and our own conferences. They give us the space to share
experiences and seek common solutions. We need to believe in
ourselves and each other as women and organise around our demands.

These ideas provided the background for a new surge of interest in positive action for women. There were practical arguments in favour too. Even if equal opportunities exist in theory, few women can take them up in practice. Family duties hold them back or they lack the necessary training or experience. Positive steps are necessary to try and redress the balance.

In trade unions, positive action has taken many forms:
* reserved women's seats on executives and other bodies
* women's conferences
* women's advisory committees, both nationally and regionally
* women-only training courses for shop stewards
* the appointment of national women's officers

Many of these are recommended in the TUC Charter for Women in Unions. This document was drawn up by the women's advisory committee of the TUC in 1979, and has helped to spread ideas about positive action.

What does positive action achieve? Does it help more women to become active? Does it alter attitudes towards women or change negotiating priorities? Answers to these questions can be found in the experience of three forms of positive action: reserved seats on union executives; women's advisory committees; and women-only training courses.

Giving up their seats to the ladies

Reserved seats for women are not a new idea. The general council of the TUC has had two seats for the women workers' group since its formation in 1920, thanks to the National Federation of Women Workers. At that time, many unions did not admit women into membership. Many women workers had no choice but to form unions of their own. To make sure women had a voice at the top, they campaigned successfully for two seats on the general council. The seats have survived the intervening 60 years, though the idea was not taken up elsewhere.

Recently it has returned with vigour. NUPE was one of the first to revive the idea when the union added five women's seats to its executive in 1975. The impetus did not come from the membership, but from an academic study into the union's structure. The posts are elected by the membership; each woman represents female interests in two of NUPE's ten divisions.

Supporters of positive action regard NUPE as a success story. They hoped the reserved seats would encourage women to stand for other executive posts. In fact, three other women have since been elected to NUPE's 25-person executive, making a total of eight—a

TUC Charter

Equality for women within trade unions

Commended by the General Council of the Trades Union Congress 'to all union executives and committees . . . for the integration of women within trade unions at all levels'. Endorsed by Congress, 1979.

1 The National Executive Committee of the union should publicly declare to all its members the commitment of the union to involving women members in the activities of the union at all levels.

2 The structure of the union should be examined to see whether it prevents women from reaching the decision-making bodies.

3 Where there are large women's memberships but no women on the decision-making bodies special provision should be made to ensure that women's views are represented, either through the creation of additional seats or by co-option.

4 The National Executive Committee of each union should consider the desirability of setting up advisory committees within its constitutional machinery to ensure that the special interests of its women members are protected.

5 Similar committees at regional, divisional, and district level could also assist by encouraging the active involvement of women in the general activities of the union.

6 Efforts should be made to include in collective agreements provision for time off without loss of pay to attend branch meetings during working hours where that is practicable.

7 Where it is not practicable to hold meetings during working hours every effort should be made to provide child-care facilities for use by either parent.

8 Child-care facilities, for use by either parent, should be provided at all district, divisional and regional meetings and particularly at the union's annual conference, and for training courses organised by the union.

9 Although it may be open to any members of either sex to go to union training courses, special encouragement should be given to women to attend.

10 The content of journals and other union publications should be presented in non-sexist terms.

great advance on 1973 when there were no women at all.

But are reserved seats just a case of token women? There is always the danger of having a small minority who are tolerated but whose ideas make little progress. Some women oppose the idea of reserved seats for this reason. To offset the risk it is important to have, like NUPE, a substantial number of reserved seats. Two voices are easily lost in a large committee. Five can be more persistent. Women have been trying for years to increase the number of women's seats on the general council of the TUC (which has 41 members). Congress agreed in 1981 to increase the number from two to five—an improvement but still less than the seven women wanted. The Scottish TUC, a smaller body, had no reserved seats before 1981. A conference decision introduced two women's seats, reflecting a new mood in favour of positive action.

Even if reserved seats smack of tokenism, they are one way of making sure that women's voices are heard on executive bodies. Also, the people involved can provide useful national leadership for women. But it would be unwise to view reserved seats as a final solution to women's under-representation. They are likely to be most effective as one part of a broader programme of positive action which would aim to promote more women into non-reserved seats as well.

Alternative networks for women

Equal opportunity committees, equality working parties, women's advisory committee—all these aim to promote the interests of women in the union concerned. The TUC has had a women's advisory committee since 1931. Some unions have had them for years; others are in the process of setting them up.

What is the value of these committees? One ASTMS activist explained that her committee is a focus for 'an alternative network for women in the union'. Active women in some parts of the country find themselves isolated in old-fashioned branches. Others have exhausting national posts. For all of them, getting together through a women's committee can be personally and politically supportive. Like a women's conference, it re-charges run-down feminist batteries, builds up friendships and gives women the energy to carry on. In this way women are building networks in unions, an alternative to the brotherhood that keeps men going. For example, one woman, active in the NUJ, says that:

> There is a very positive attitude I see emerging from the women's movement and which has affected me most: the example and support of other women on a very personal level has

been crucial.

A women's committee may be the only body at a national level in a union where women know their concerns will always be treated seriously. Like the TUC women's conference, the committees have influenced policy in many important areas—including abortion, maternity rights, childcare, new technology and fighting cutbacks. Many have done surveys of women in the union and have used the results as a springboard for more positive action. They have orga- nised training courses, written pamphlets and galvanised their unions into running women's conferences.

But there are still problems. Some equality committees are mixed and lack the special atmosphere of those that are made up of women only. Women's committees may be mistrusted by the men who run the union. In the NUJ, there have been several vigorous attempts to get rid of the Equality Working Party. Or the committee may be isolated from the mainstream of union affairs. This is a tricky dilem- ma to solve. A women's committee wants to be well integrated into the union structure to give it as much power as possible. On the other hand, if the aim is not simply to achieve a superficial equality, but to challenge male norms and develop women's interests, then the com- mittee needs some freedom from the constraints of the structure. Earlier (pp. 28–30, above), we saw how an inaugural meeting of a women's committee without this freedom went badly wrong. Instead of the lively and supportive few hours it might have been, it was a wishy-washy, rather boring event. The union did not let it have a life of its own. It was smothered before it was even born.

Such committees enable the union to say, 'Yes, we're interested in equality—look, we have women's advisory committees'. But they will probably see precious little improvement in women's participa- tion. And a women's committee, however good, cannot work mira- cles on its own. Like reserved seats, it needs to be part of a bigger action plan for women: a plan for training schools and conferences, backed up by resources, publications and staff time.

Few unions have all of these. NALGO has equality committees, but is wary of women-only training and refuses to send delegates to the TUC women's conference. NUPE has reserved seats and women's courses but no women's advisory committee (though one is now promised). The TGWU has a patchy coverage of regional women's committees, but nothing at a national level and no women on its executive. As always, piecemeal approaches give piecemeal results. A union which takes positive action seriously, carefully involving everyone from the smallest branches to the most powerful committees stands to reap the rewards of growing energy and enthusiasm from its female membership. Unions which take half-hearted measures will find that the results are equally half-hearted. They will flop, leaving women frustrated and annoyed.

'I realise I'm not on my own'

One of the most sparkling developments of the past few years has been the advent of women-only courses for shop stewards and staff representatives. A course may be a single weekend or a full week; it may be organised by an individual union or through the TUC's education service. Women from the shop floor have a chance to relax in the company of other female shop stewards and talk over their union problems. The result is often an electric, even euphoric, atmosphere. Confidence leaps forward in a few days, there is a lot of laughter as anxiety and timidity is released, and people go home exhausted and full of new ideas. This may sound a hopelessly exaggerated picture. But it is surprisingly close to reality and will be familiar to women who have experienced the 'high' of an all-women event. Just listen to comments from shop stewards on women's courses in Newcastle upon Tyne:

> The three days made me realise I am not on my own with my views and am not a neurotic deviant!

> A lot of things have been clarified in my own mind and it has been a joy to watch the other women actually blossoming under the support of the group.

> Well, I think I would not be frightened to bring a point forward now as I have gained confidence at these meetings what I did not have before.

To many of the shop stewards, being in a group of women feels quite natural as they work in all-female jobs. But it is a new experience in their *union* activity, and most love it.

> At least one can put forward one's feelings and ideas without feeling silly in front of men.

> Being on an all-women course I found it easier to talk, and being so green about union matters I was not embarrassed as I would have been if men had been present.

> I would have come on a mixed course, but perhaps would have taken a less active part.

> This course being all women builds one's confidence.

The critics of women's courses feared they would weaken the trade unions by separating women from men. Experience has shown the courses to have the opposite effect. A few days in an all-women class can be the confidence-booster and energy-giver a shop steward needs to cope with the demands of mixed union meetings. She has discovered that her views of the world as a woman can be taken seriously in a union context. As a result she is better prepared to take her place as an active trade unionist.

> I feel I have been prepared for further courses now. I could attend a mixed course and 'hold my own'.

> When I found out this was an all-women's course I was annoyed, believing as I do that there is too much segregation in the trade unions. However I feel now I was wrong. The advantages do outweigh the disadvantages because the women on the course gained confidence and were more at ease. The integration should follow on naturally upon the confidence and knowledge gained.

> Before this I was a little lukewarm about going further in the union but now it seems that I might be as capable as anyone.

After a three day course for APEX staff representatives, one woman left with a cheery wave to the others, saying 'See you all on the national executive!'

Women's courses must not be misunderstood. They are not remedial classes to give the ladies a chance to catch up a bit before joining the men on a real shop stewards course. On the contrary, the classes are important in their own right. It is not a question of trying to imitate male colleagues. The aim is to give women a chance to increase their knowledge and skills, and to hammer out their own approach as women trade unionists.

Positive action results in a challenge to established practices. As women become active and change, union procedures and methods will have to change too. It is little use having women's courses unless a union is also prepared to organise childcare, re-arrange meeting times, open up agendas and act against sexism. The need for all these is, if anything, increasing at the moment. As Patricia Leman, a member of the TUC women's advisory committee, wrote in the NATFHE Journal in February 1982:

> In the present climate of attacks on the right of women to work we need, more than ever, channels such as the women's advisory committee which encourage woman's voice to be heard and her

interests served within the trade union movement.

Forwards or backwards?

At the same time as ideas about positive action in unions are gaining ground, progress towards equal opportunities for women at work is very slow. As the recession bites, women are trying hard to hold on to what they already have and do not have a lot of energy left to fight for further advances.

Women workers are affected by all the major problems of today. Cutbacks, industrial decline and unemployment present massive problems to trade unions. The early eighties is proving to be a very unhappy period for the trade-union movement in general, and for women in particular. Bargaining power has been seriously eroded by the poor economic situation and an unsympathetic political climate. A union that prides itself on having a high degree of control over working conditions and wage levels can find itself suddenly powerless when it comes to fighting redundancies or a threatened closure. The traditional strike weapon is not much use at such times. As for groups of women workers whose union organisation is weak or non-existent, they are more vulnerable still.

So is there a danger of losing some of the gains of the seventies? The gap between men's and women's pay is opening out again. Jobs are disappearing. Job segregation is increasing in those that remain. And all this is happening in the context of a highly reactionary government whose policies are making it harder for women to stay in employment. Maternity rights were reduced in the Employment Act of 1980, and cutbacks in the welfare state have forced many women to return home to care for dependents.

Simple ideas about equality are not enough to counter the effect of these developments on women. As well as a fight-back, symbolised by the successful Lee Jeans occupation in Scotland, something more is needed—a commitment to positive action for women at work. Positive action means looking below the surface to reach a deeper understanding of women's position in society. We learned in the seventies that removing discrimination is not enough. Women are all too often still trapped in stereotyped roles which prevent them from making choices about their lives. Some are tied down by family pressures and the reduction of support facilities. Others are sexually harassed. Many more are held back because employers, and society in general, continuously re-inforce the lesson they learnt as little girls—that women are expected to be more passive, have less ambition and earn less than men. And that they should accept their secondary status in the labour force because home-making and motherhood should be their main vocations in life.

Positive action is about getting rid of the stereotypes by uncovering the factors which maintain them and counter-acting them. For trade unions it means action on two levels—with the employer, and in the political sphere.

Action at work

In virtually every company where employers blithely say, 'Oh yes, we have equal opportunities here', real inequality still exists. Women stay at the bottom of the pile, men rise to the top. The clerical 'girls' service the male bosses. Skilled fitters and maintenance men earn double the wages of the shop-floor women. The usual story.

Positive action starts with examining the picture in detail. Analysing it—finding who is in which job, how they got there and where they are heading. Then asking questions. Why is this grade all women? What are the criteria for promotion? How many men and women have been on training courses? Why so few women? It entails going over job descriptions to weed out indirect discrimination against women. Do salespersons really need to move at a moment's notice? Are rigid working hours necessary? Would two years experience do instead of five?

Management and unions then have to get their heads together to work out what to do to overcome women's disadvantages. This takes time and energy, and it is vital that women are involved in the decision-making. The whole exercise will be a farce unless both sides genuinely want it to succeed. Management will have to change personnel practices; train interviewers in non-sexist techniques; remove unnecessary qualifications from job descriptions; and plan advertisements to encourage women to apply. Unions will have to be prepared to re-negotiate grading schemes, and build equal opportunities clauses into collective agreements. More difficult still, they will have to educate their members to accept change.

Breaking the circle

But even this is not enough to break the vicious circle of women's work. In our society servicing other people's needs is regarded as women's work. The work is given low value. At home, it is unpaid; in a job, it is low paid. Because of its low value, men don't want to do it, so it remains women's work. Men's and women's work stay separated. The circle is complete.

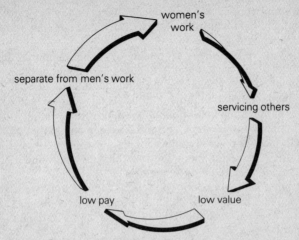

women's
work

separate from men's work

servicing others

low pay   low value

Breaking the circle will need a massive effort to overturn existing stereotypes and radically re-think working practices. The women's movement is, of course, essential in this process as a source of ideas and a model for alternative ways of organising. For the trade unions, we can draw together some key policies for positive action campaigns.

* *Reduced working time.* Reduced working hours that are *not* made up with more overtime, but which free men and women to share domestic tasks and childcare. The TUC is backing the campaign for a shorter working week. Most progress has been made in white-collar jobs. Employers are proving to be very reluctant to reduce working time for shop-floor workers. Related union aims include longer holidays, regular sabbatical years and earlier retirement.

* *A fair deal for part-timers.* Giving part-timers the same rights and conditions as full-timers. Making many more jobs available on a part-time basis, perhaps through job-sharing. Some employers now accept job-sharing, mostly as a result of pressure from individual applicants. Unions generally have not given priority to this issue.

* *Parents' rights.* Round-the-clock nursery facilities which are good for children and good for parents too. Extended maternity and paternity leave. Time off to look after sick dependents. Most unions with large female memberships now have model maternity agreements—but negotiating them is a different matter. Paternity leave and family responsibilities leave still seem to be low on the agenda.

* *Housework and childcare for all*. To get away from the idea that they are only women's work. When will we see this as a real trade-union issue?

* *Realistic child benefit*. To remove arguments about the family wage from wage bargaining. To reduce poverty in families with dependent children. This area demands far more attention from unions than it receives at present. The debate about the family wage needs to be stirred up in the trade-union movement.

* *Training for women*. Courses for women and girls in all areas of work, including non-traditional skills and computer-based jobs. Unions need to exert more pressure on employers and training bodies to run special courses for women.

* *Revised pay structures*. To re-value 'female' work, reduce differentials, and bring women's wages up to the level of men's. This will be a long, hard fight, and the first battle has to be fought inside the unions themselves.

Little progress towards these aims will be made until the trade-union movement better reflects women's interests. Positive action at work goes hand-in-hand with positive action in unions. It is essential that women should play a fuller part in union affairs. And that women have the chance to shape trade unionism to suit their own needs.

Women will carry on fighting for what they want with or without trade unions. But there is little doubt that a union is the best vehicle for achieving change at work. The trade-union movement can also be a powerful political force in support of women's demands.

Are the unions up to the challenge? Will they take positive action seriously? Will they understand how the movement as a whole can grow stronger, more responsive and more democratic through women's contribution? Are men prepared to share power? One thing *is* certain. Women trade unionists will keep on working hard to make sure their sisters stay involved and that unions do change. Theirs is not a new struggle, and it is one that will undoubtedly carry on for many years. Optimism has always prevailed somehow. Women believe in what they are doing and go on finding the energy to carry on. This has been true throughout the history of women in trade unions.

Remembering this, there can be no better note on which to end than to recall (from *My Song Is My Own*) the enthusiasm expressed by women on strike in 1911 at the Idris soft drinks factory:

Now then girls all join the union
   Whatever you may be,
In pickles, jam, or chocolate
   Or packing pounds of tea.
For we all want better wages
   And this is what we say—
We're out to right the wrong, and
   Now we shan't be long,
Hip hurray! Hip hurray!

A Guide to Reading

Chapter 1. Many unions publish pamphlets and information for women members. The Transport and General Workers Union *Women's Handbook* is one example. The Counter Information Services anti-report on *Women in the Eighties* is a useful summary of many aspects of women's lives. *Only Halfway to Paradise* by Elizabeth Wilson, Tavistock 1980, is a very good book on women in post-war Britain. For an excellent introduction to the whole area, *Women at Work* by Chris Aldred, Pan 1981, is highly recommended. Another book with the same title, by Lindsay Mackie and Polly Patullo, Tavistock 1977, is a very readable account of women's work. Two magazines which contain articles and news about women and unions are the feminist monthly *Spare Rib,* and *Women's Voice*.

Chapter 2. Useful facts and figures can be found in *Women, Work and Trade Union Organisation* by Judith Hunt and Shelley Adams, 1980, a pamphlet published by the Workers Educational Association. *The Role of Trade Unions in the Promotion of Equal Opportunities* by Valerie Ellis, Equal Opportunities Commission 1981, provides a review of the literature on women and trade unions. Anna Pollert's *Girls, Wives, Factory Lives*, Macmillan 1981, is a fascinating account of women working in a tobacco factory. *Man Made Language* by Dale Spender, Routledge & Kegan Paul 1980, is an eye-opening feminist analysis of the use of language.

Chapter 4. For a stimulating discussion of feminist and traditional views of work, Virginia Navarro's *Women's Work, Men's Work*, Marion Boyars 1980, is well worth a look. Olive Schreiner's *Women and Labour*, first published in 1911, was re-issued by Virago in 1978 and is still fresh and interesting. *Hear This Brother—Women Workers and Trade Union Power* by Anna Coote and Peter Kellner, New Statesman 1981, gives a clear overview of women's role in trade unions. Anna Coote's most recent book, *Sweet Freedom*, written with Beatrice Campbell, Picador 1982, is a descriptive history of the women's movement and has a chapter on the unions.

Several other worthwhile books have also recently been republished by Virago: *Women Workers and the Industrial Revolution*, Ivy Pinchbeck's classic about the effect of industrialisation on women (1980) and *Maternity: Letters from Working Women* (1976) and *Life As We Have Known It* (1977), both edited by Margaret Llewelyn-Davies of the Women's Cooperative Guild. A valuable guide to current maternity law is provided in Jean Coussins' *Maternity Rights for Working Women*, NCCL 1981.

Biographies of women can be both enjoyable and informative. Two particularly inspiring ones are *The Hard Way Up* by Hannah Mitchell, who described herself as a suffragist and rebel, and *The Tamarisk Tree* by Dora Russell which includes her description of the campaign for birth control. Both were published by Virago in 1977. Also from that period, the *Women's Year Book* of 1923–24 contains a wealth of detail about women's organisations and campaigns.

Turning to new technology at work, the TUC and most large unions have published booklets on this theme. Counter Information Services' *The New Technology* is a useful overview, and a number of recent books contain chapters on new technology and unemployment.

Chapter 5. Among books about the history of women and trade unions, Sarah Boston's *Women Workers and the Trade Unions*, Davis-Poynter 1980, is highly recommended as it is both readable and lively. *Hidden from History* by Sheila Rowbotham, Pluto 1973, is a more general book, and a valuable introduction to women's history. Sheila Lewenhak's *Women and Trade Unions*, Ernest Benn 1977, is a more detailed work.

Fenwomen is a delightful book about women's lives in a small village recorded by Mary Chamberlain (Virago 1977).

A number of pamphlets about the Equal Pay and Sex Discrimination Acts are available. The Department of Employment sponsored M. W. Snell, P. Glucklich and M. Povall at the London School of Economics to research *Equal Pay and Opportunities*, which is a detailed account of the implementation of the acts (Department of Employment Research Paper 20). The National Council for Civil Liberties (NCCL) has published several relevant booklets, including *The Equality Report* by Jean Coussins (1977).

My Song Is My Own, Pluto 1979, is a wonderful collection of women's songs edited by Kathy Henderson, Frankie Armstrong and Sandra Kerr.

Chapter 7. Sadie Robart's *Positive Action—The Next Step* was published by the NCCL in 1980 and deals with the subject in a practical way. To keep in touch with developments in the trade unions, it is worth looking at *Women Workers*, the annual report of the women's advisory committee of the TUC.

Charlie Clutterbuck and Tim Lang
More Than We Can Chew

Under the Common Agricultural Policy, Europe has become a landscape of butter mountains and wine lakes. Farmers produce more food every year. But much of it fails to reach those who need it, a situation that breeds ingenious schemes for dumping and recycling foodstocks.

More Than We Can Chew examines the power struggles and crazy contradictions of the modern world food economy and shows their impact on nutrition, food adulteration and factory conditions.

Charlie Clutterbuck and Tim Lang have both been farmers in the north of England. They are active in the Agricap group of the British Society for Social Responsibility in Science.

£2.50   ISBN 0 86104 501 7

Richard Minns
Take Over the City

In 1982 a row broke out about plans by the Mineworkers' Pension Fund to increase its investments in South Africa. This is just one example of the way a handful of banks, insurance companies and pension funds invest vast sums for short-term gain. They are spending other people's money – savings made through pension schemes, insurance policies and bank accounts. But do decisions made in the City benefit ordinary savers?

The Wilson Committee, set up by the 1974-79 Labour government, found no serious problems with the way the City operates. **Take Over the City** argues differently – that only public ownership of financial institutions can provide the basis for an alternative investment strategy to create jobs.

Richard Minns works for the Economic Development Unit of West Midlands County Council. He is the author of **Pension Funds and British Capitalism.**

£2.50   ISBN 0 86104 502 5

Colin Thunhurst
It Makes You Sick

Today the National Health Service is on the point of collapse and private health care schemes are burgeoning. Colin Thunhurst shows how the progressive potential of the NHS has been undermined by successive governments ever since its inception. He argues that this is a product of the society we live in – that modern capitalism creates ill-health and profits from it.

It Makes You Sick proposes policies for re-shaping and democratising the NHS: policies which go well beyond those of the Labour Party and show what a genuinely socialist system of health care might look like.

Colin Thunhurst has written extensively about health issues and is active in campaigns around the NHS in Sheffield. He is a lecturer at Sheffield Polytechnic.

£2.50   ISBN 0 86104 503 3